A MANLY GUIDE to Cool Stuff

Mantiques

by Eric Bradley

Published by

Krause Publications, a division of F+W Media, Inc.
700 East State Street • Iola, WI 54990-0001
715-445-2214 • 888-457-2873
www.krausebooks.com

To order books or other products call toll-free 1-800-258-0929
or visit us online at www.krausebooks.com

Front cover: Fishing illustration by Bill Gregg (see P. 119),
Used Cars "Safety Tested" sign (see P. 52), a Gil Elvgren calendar illustration (see P. 59),
1967 Boston Red Sox World Series pennant sold as part of the Carl Yastrzemski Pennant Collection, set of 23 pieces, $215; photo courtesy Heritage Auctions, and a Schmidt's Beer Glass Bullet Lighted Sign, circa 1930s-1940s, made by Blue Ribbon Displays, near mint condition, 14-1/2" h, $1,920; photo courtesy Morphy Auctions.
Back cover: Beacon Security Gasoline sign (see P. 60), Three Stooges poster (see P. 20),
a Reynolds Yater Pocket Rocket surfboard (see P. 46),
and a 1935 Indian Chief motorcycle (see P. 57).

ISBN-13: 978-1-4402-3986-1
ISBN-10: 1-4402-3986-X

Designed by Sharon Bartsch
Edited by Kristine Manty

Printed in China

TO MY PARENTS, DAVID AND KAREN, FOR FILLING OUR HOME WITH LAUGHTER AND FANTASTIC THINGS.

Acknowledgments

Without the help and inspiration of the following friends, colleagues, and fellow manti-quers, this book wouldn't have been written: Paul Kennedy, Kristine Manty, Debbie Rexing, Noah Fleisher, Greg Holman, John Dale Beety, Clarence Blanchard, Steve Yauch, John Loftis, Gretchen Bell, Jacques & Kelli van Gool, Kristen Schultz, Dan Matthews, Dan Morphy, Tema Zerbe, Lisa Oakes, Scott Bass, Patrick Hogan, Maria Burdick, Laura Gonzales, Stan Van Etten, Karen Knapstein, Antoinette Rahn, Alyssa Duffy, Brian Williams, Sean Hinz, and photographers Joaquin Andrew and Jeffrey Padgett.

Special thanks to my wife, Kelly, and our children, Patrick, Olivia, and Megan, for their patience and support.

CONTENTS

MANTIQUES

FUELED BY TESTOSTERONE AND ATTITUDE

Robert Owen, left, and Compton Creel own DFW M'antiques and Neat Stuff in Dallas. The two are part of a nationwide trend marketing swell collectibles to guys.

uys tend to think of "antiques" as a euphemism for stuffy, musty, dainty, shatter-prone headaches with no practical purpose in today's modern world. Other than giving us one more thing to dust, "antiques" just sit somewhere being, well, brown.

Mantiques, on the other hand, are complete opposites. Hunting down mantiques gives you the rare occasion in your life to hear someone say, "That's an awesome ball of twine!" and sincerely mean it.

If you think about the premise of most of the "found money" collecting television shows dominating every channel, it's easy to see why they all star men. Mantiques are fun and, as it turns out, pretty lucrative. The trend isn't limited to American television; dealers and collectors in Europe are also celebrating the renewed attention to items that appeal to men. U.S. auction houses are developing the trend as well, with Heritage Auctions, the world's largest collectibles auctioneer, and where I happily work, now holding a Gentleman Collector auction every year.

Talk about divine intervention. This bible was in the pocket of Pvt. Edwin C. Hall of the 10th Vermont Vol. Inf. when it was struck by a Confederate "minie ball" at the Battle of Sailor's Creek on April 6, 1865. It saved his life and so moved Private Hall that he kept the bible for 33 years before sending it off to a museum. It was sold at auction for $15,535.

Although the name "mantiques" to describe items appealing to guys has existed for about 30 years, the concept of the mantique is ancient. When they weren't chasing mammoths off cliffs, our ancestors were saving interesting stones, carving ivory tusks, or trading with other tribes. Why go through the trouble? The dude with the coolest stuff was seen as better able to care for offspring or lead the tribe to greatness. From Alibaba's lamp to Luke Skywalker's lightsaber (it is a hand me down, remember), mantiques are in our DNA.

Fast forward to the 21st century and we've got television shows devoted to them, for crying out loud. The mantiques movement is big and chances are you're already a part of it.

Five Reasons You're Into Mantiques

 MANTIQUES ARE FUNKY, UNIQUE, AND BITCHIN' – AND RARELY MATCH

Bikes. Toys. Tools. Weapons. Fossils. Cars. Jukeboxes. Motorcycles. Taxidermy bullfrogs playing poker. Mantiques are collectibles pursued by a new generation of men eager to fill their homes with items that defy collecting traditions and challenge the imagination.

"It is a trend with a long history," says Ben Pentreath, architectural designer, collector, and owner of Albion Prints in London. "There have always been cabinets of curiosities and natural history collections. Men have never stopped collecting. We're just seeing the modern version."

A mantiques collector isn't fooled by the words "limited edition," "collector's edition," or "collect the whole set." No way. Mantiques have substance. They are testaments to a man's individuality, his sense of design, and his innate talent at getting his buddies to shout, "Now THAT is cool! Where did you get it? It looks great in here!"

Some collectors set a course to acquire an entire series of one object. They work to corner a market by owning every available example of something in the best condition possible. A mantiques collector takes a more casual route.

② MANTIQUES COLLECTORS LIKE TO GO ON ADVENTURES

To them, the pursuit defines the collection, rather than the collection defining the pursuit. Maybe Ralph Waldo Emerson should have said, "Mantiques are a journey, not a destination." Mantiques give you a reason to meet people. Mantiques gets you out of your house and out of your comfort zone. Sign out of Facebook. Turn off your phone. The people you meet along the way make the journey worth the effort.

③ PEOPLE WHO COLLECT MANTIQUES ARE GOOD COMPANY

Here's a secret: Most major league collectors chase mantiques. Tom Hanks (who doesn't want to have a beer with Tom Hanks?!) collects vintage typewriters. Dan Aykroyd collects police badges. Frank Sinatra collected model trains. Phil Collins collects stuff relating to The Alamo. Even Leonardo DiCaprio collected vintage action figures. You meet people who are like you—or better yet—people who are nothing at all like you. You share drinks, swap stories about your finds, and learn facts about stuff you like.

④ PEOPLE WHO SELL MANTIQUES ARE AS STRANGE AND AS AWESOME AS THE OBJECTS THEY SELL

When Robert Owen and Compton Creel opened their new shop in Dallas' Oak Cliff neighborhood in 2011, they knew what they wanted to call it: M'antiques and Neat Stuff. They also knew how to set it apart from other antiques stores in the city: free beer. "The first thing I do after thanking a customer for

This shopper spotted at Massachusetts' mega Brimfield Antiques Show knows what's important in life. The shirt is courtesy CollectorsWeekly.com.

Customers at DFW M'Antiques are treated to free suds on tap.

Robert Owen, a partner in DFW M'Antiques, collects and sells antique photography. The most collectible daguerreotypes, ambrotypes, tintypes, carte de visites and cabinet cards are large and feature subjects posing with guns and knives.

coming in is ask him if he wants a beer. There's no law that says you can't look at cool stuff while holding a cold beer," Compton says.

The front of his store has a counter, a cash register, and a kegerator built into a '50s fridge with plenty of iced suds on tap. What's the specialty in the shop? "Anything and everything a man wants to own that's not in my wife's collection. We've got rusty traps, nude paintings, and turtle shells and neat stuff. We love it all."

This leads us to the final point.

5 MANTIQUES MAKE YOU SMART

Mantiques collectors also collect stories to go along with their cool stuff. Do you know why collectors like $10 gold coins issued in the 1850s by Moffit & Co.? When the U.S. Treasury ignored Californians' pleas to

An 1852 $10 Moffat & Co. coin in this condition (12 PCGS) is valued at about $3,500. It could also be worth a free drink.

issue coins worth less than $50, the ballsy of-ficers at Moffat uttered a hearty "WTF?!" and issued its own $10 gold pieces. The coins were so trusted by businesses and citizens that the company churned out more denominations. Eventually the company evolved into the offi-cial United States Mint in San Francisco, which is still in operation today. That fact alone should get you a free drink in any bar in America.

About this book

As the title says, think of this book as a guide to a world of mantiques. I have to admit, how-ever, that it's a small guide because there are far too many mantiques categories to fit into one book. I've chosen a selection of the most popular things collected today and available nearly anywhere you live. It might be tough to find fishing lures in the heart of New York, but consider that a cue that it's time for a road trip. Obviously, these categories are in no means a complete list of what you can collect. I've met hundreds of collectors who were absolutely fanatical about everything from bottles to cuf-flinks to Art Deco clocks and even sexy Am-phora porcelain. What you'll find here, how-ever, is a listing of some more popular stuff and some facts on why they remain so. This may come in handy when you start selling parts of your collection as you mature as a collector. Every collector should be a seller for two reasons:

This combination clock and barometer looks like a modern day Steampunk creation, but It dates to 1885 and is attributed to Guilmet of Paris, a well-known maker of novelty clocks. It was likely made to pay respect to the steam engine. It sold at auction for $14,340.

1. It prevents the American Psychiatric Association from diagnosing you as a hoarder.
2. It's the easiest way to invest in your collection and keep it separate from your finances.

I've heard horror stories when mantiques collectors get bit by "the bug" and do not keep their collections outside their bills. It can have tragic results for mortgages, credit scores, and even relationships.

The collections featured herein are in dens, garages, or take up entire homes across the nation. Some chapters have profiles on collectors themselves and following each profile, there is a "Get the Look" section that features a selection of mantiques that would be at home in each collection, should you be interested in starting a similar one or adding to one you already have.

I tried to let my conscience be my guide. While most of these are top examples, don't let

In DFW M'Antiques, you can find a EA-250 Riviera Epiphone electric guitar, circa 1970-74, for $450 and a signal generator from a laboratory for $98.

the prices intimidate you. They are fair market values from an auction setting, so don't be surprised if you find a similar piece priced a bit more or less depending on where you find it. And as you'll learn, most mantiques collectors find items for their collections through unconventional means, such as online, pickers, or even by just driving through neighborhoods during trash pick-up nights.

There are no rules when it comes to mantiques and, in some cases, the crazier the grouping, the more personality it has. A friend of mine devotes his collection to a group of mantiques called New Old Stock, or NOS, for those in the hobby. His collection didn't fit among his larger effort—which focused on vintage coin-op slot machines and one-armed bandits—so he plastered the walls of a guest bathroom in the basement with vintage 1950s tin toys, 1970s character toothbrushes, and a shelf full of vintage condom tins. Hey, whatever floats your boat.

Buy what you want. Your collection will look great in the end.

Mantiques Invading the Nation

America is in the grip of a mantiques epidemic. From coast to coast, more than a dozen shops have opened during the last decade, all using some variation on the word "mantiques." They may share the same name and the same love for weird and off-beat objects, but the guys behind these shops are as unique as they come.

The first true shop to use the name "mantiques" opened in the 1970s in New York by two women, said Cory Margolis, a second-generation dealer/picker, who kept the ladies supplied with barware, smoking items, and other gentlemen luxury accessories. When one of the partners passed away, Cory stepped in and bought the business in 2003. Mantiques Modern is

MANTIQUES ROAD TRIP

ARIZONA
Mancave Mantiques
Glendale, AZ

CALIFORNIA
Mantiques Vintage Radios
Santee, CA

Mantiques
Fremont, CA

San Pedro Mantiques
San Pedro, CA

COLORADO
Mantiques
Florence, CO

MINNESOTA
Jim's "MAN"tiques
Saint Charles, MN

NEW HAMPSHIRE
MANTIQUERS
Rochester, NH

NEW YORK
Mantiques Modern
New York, NY

NORTH CAROLINA
MANtiques
Cashiers, NC

OHIO
Mantiques
Elmore, OH

TEXAS
DFW M'Antiques
Dallas, TX

Texas Coin and Mantiques
Lufkin, TX

WASHINGTON
Mantiques Unlimited
Auburn, WA

WISCONSIN
Mantiques
Janesville, WI

**Double D Mantiques
and Collectibles**
Milwaukee, WI

This Tonka vehicle is one of the items for sale at Mantiques of Janesville, WI.

Elvis stands watch over the Mantiques shop of Fremont, CA.

Mantiques Modern's polished instrument panel from an actual 1940s bomber.

now one of the hottest vintage-related businesses in the country.

The shop, located on West 22nd Street in New York, served as headquarters as Cory set up at antiques shows up and down the East Coast and added up-scale merchandise to websites such as 1stdibs.com. "We mainly sell to interior designers and other high-end retailers," Cory said. "We're pickers with a shop, but taste makers of sorts."

Mantiques Modern's inventory ranges from a highly polished instrument panel from an actual 1940s bomber to a giant, leather rhinoceros created for Abercrombie in the 1940s, back when it was known as a

source for sporting goods, rather than as a source for nude guys who need a sandwich. But vintage finds from luxury brand names is the shop's specialty. Inventory comes from fellow pickers and fleas across New England and Europe. Inevitably, items turn up in window displays at Bergdorf Goodman and other high-end retailers.

The appearance of guy-themed mantiques shops across the nation can be partially attributed to the arrival of television reality shows devoted to pickers and pawn shops. But like Mantiques Modern, most shop owners say their real motivation had to do with filling a niche.

Bill Paesano and Will Murphy (yeah, Bill and Will, they hear that often), owners of Mantiquers of Rochester, NH, focus on the odd and unique items that can take your man cavee up a notch. They also specialize in signs.

The MANtiques shop of San Pedro, California.

Ernie Scarano, owner of Mantiques of Elmore, Ohio, opened his shop seven years ago to bring unusual items to market. "I sell all manly stuff," he says. "Over the years, I've sold several chain gang uniforms, World War II cipher machines, and a $20 bill from John Dillinger's October 23, 1933 bank robbery. Currently, I have Eva Braun's panties!" (See page 71.)

As if running Mantiques isn't enough, Ernie opened his own whiskey distillery in Fremont, Ohio, in 2010. The Ernest Scarano Distillery, named after his father, Ernie, Sr., will be selling bottles of a rye whisky blend he's branded Old Homicide. The first bottles should be available in mid-2014. Between the two locations, Ernie stays pretty busy and until the whiskey takes off, his attention is still focused on "tools, vintage cigarette packs, U-boat leather coveralls … just a ton of guy stuff."

The term mantiques is just far enough removed from the ordinarily teacup-infused word "antiques" to attract young entrepreneurs, too. Thirty-somethings Bill Paesano and his partner, Will Murphy, specialize in decking out man caves, recreation and media rooms and even offices as co-owners of

Mantiquers and PorcelainNeonSigns.com of Rochester, New Hampshire. The two quit their stable and profitable jobs to haggle, prowl junkyards, and salvage in the rain.

"We have CEOs, CFOs, and other real important people asking us to find cool things for them," Bill says. "We have so many orders, we can barely keep up. Guys are always looking for signs and cool stuff."

Collectors' insatiable appetites for the weird and unusual is the No. 1 reason Compton Creel and Robert Owen say DFW M'Antiques has grown every month since opening in Dallas' hip Bishop Arts District in 2011. The 2,500-square-foot group mall is packed with oddities including pinball machines, cannons, and the front end of a GMC pickup truck. "We make it a place for guys to just hang out," Owen said.

The shop doubles as a studio where he paints toy soldiers, and stores his extensive collection after a career in the toy business.

A line from their television commercial sums up every mantiques shop across the nation: "If you're looking for a classic antique for your loved one in the retirement home, oh man, did you come to the wrong place!"

Five Mantiques You Shouldn't Legally Be Allowed to Own

Once you've headed down the path to mantiques obsession, you may wonder if there's any limit to what you can and can't collect. After all, one of the central tenants of a mantique is that rules don't count. You'd be surprised at the things you're legally allowed to buy, sell, or trade in the realm of mantiques. The following are all legally obtainable collectibles that would be an enviable addition to anyone's collection.

$2,270

Trinitite Paperweight

Some men use pretty glass spheres as a paperweight. A mantiques collector uses what's left of liquefied radioactive desert sand left over from an atomic blast. This 1-1/4" plastic paperweight contains a 5/8" specimen of Trinitite. This is the end product after an atomic blast causes sand on the surface of ground zero to be drawn up into the nuclear fireball and then fall in liquid form like rain. Yeah, you heard me. Military personnel gathered samples after the July 16, 1945 blast at Alamogordo, New Mexico, and some were sold as novelties to mineral collectors.

Marilyn Monroe Chest X-Ray   **$4,687**

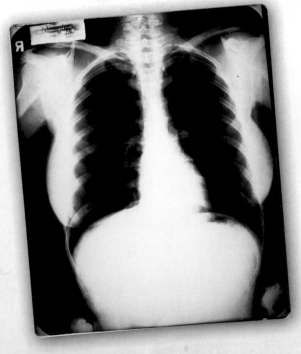

Few men got close to Marilyn Monroe's heart, but this 1954-era copy of her original chest X-ray gets you pretty darn close. This was likely made for another doctor's use and clearly shows the star's sternum, ribcage, and an outline of her breasts, as she rests her hands on her hips. Va va va voom.

$5,975 Franklin D. Roosevelt's Cocktail Shaker

When he wasn't salvaging the American economy from the worst economic crisis in its history or saving the planet from the Nazi scourge, our 36th president liked to tip a few back like the rest of us. This personally owned cocktail shaker from his home at Top Hill Cottage was gifted to the president by his Attorney General in 1938. It probably got plenty of use just so he could keep up with his good friend and fellow tippler Winston Churchill. Rather than molder away inside some museum, the shaker was sold at auction in 2012.

Fort Knox Bullion Depository Original Blueprints

$6,572   You read that right. Evidently, the U.S. Treasury Department spent all of its time building a pistol range in the basement of Fort Knox Bullion Depository and none of its time keeping track of the blueprints to the place! The vault of the Fort Knox Bullion Depository holds much of the United States' gold reserves. The depository, located approximately 30 miles southwest of Louisville, KY, on a site which was formerly a part of the Fort Knox military reservation, was completed in December 1936 at a cost of $560,000. According to these original blueprints, which were sold at auction in 2009, the vault door alone weighs more than 20 tons and is surrounded by 16,500 square feet of granite and more than 670 tons of structural steel. Oh, and that pistol range? That's no joke. The range is actually on the plans.

The Belly Gun $418

Around 1850, a firearms craftsman designed and built a pistol that straps to your belly. Why he built it is lost to history, but his contraption is a dazzling mix of ingenuity. Unique in every way, the "gun" is a 2-7/8" x 6-3/4" iron plate mounted on a thick, 3 3/8" wide leather belt with two heavy copper rivets for tying it closed at the back. Mounted on the plate is a unique percussion lock with 1-3/8" .50 caliber

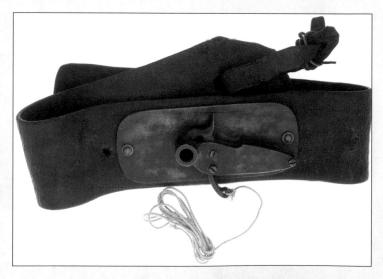

smoothbore mounted perpendicular to it. The lock is fitted with a "trigger" at the bottom with a hole drilled through it to accept a cord that was pulled to fire it. There is plenty to want in this mantique.

YOU
PAY FOR
THE
DRINKS...
THEY
DO
THE **REST!**

the cocktail
Hostesses

ADULTS ONLY

THEY'RE HERE TO PLEASE YOU!

Starring: RENEÉ BOND · TERRI JOHNSON · LYNN HARRIS · KATHY HILTON · FORMAN SHANE

Produced and Directed by A.C. STEPHEN

RELEASED BY SCA DISTRIBUTORS

IN EASTMANCOLOR   AN A-A PRODUCTION

BOTTOMS UP
COLLECTING VINTAGE BARWARE

Setting up a home bar is so mainstream now that even big box retailers and two-bit department stores offer you a range of "bar tools and accessories" to display your olives and shake your martinis. We get it! It's fashionable to drink at home, but where's the personality? How much fake rattan cane can people tolerate before they bust out and get the cool stuff?!

A proper home bar needs three things: Booze. Friends. Crazy shit on the walls. Take away any one of those things and your bar is kinda just a sad place to get drunk at home. That's not what you're looking for. You're looking for a great place to hang with friends, maybe have a rare cigarette, and shoot the bull over a few cocktails or a beer and otherwise unwind. Remember: A gentleman always hides the girly glasses with melt-away negligees behind the bar and only pulls them out when mixed company leaves.

Adding any of the following mantiques to your home bar instantly gives you permission to have that one extra beer that takes the edge off the world. These things encourage you to invite your friends over for a generously strong cocktail and some hearty laughs at the screwball stuff you found for your space. Breweriana and vintage barware hold their value extremely well. When the time comes to swap them out of your collection, you have a better-than-average chance to make a few bucks on the deal.

OPPOSITE PAGE: The perfect poster for your home bar, this one sheet is for the sexploitation flick *The Cocktail Hostesses*, SCA, 1973, starring Renee Bond and Rick Cassidy. It measures 28" x 42" and sold for $32 at auction.

Made of porcelain by O'Hayle of Chicago, this sign was probably produced when the company was renamed Indianapolis Brewing in 1935 just after prohibition. It measures 16" x 7" and sold for $460.

WE SELL DUESSELDORFER BEER
INDIANAPOLIS BREWING CO.

RULES OF THUMB

1. Beer memorabilia will hold its value better than, say, whiskey memorabilia. Consider joining the National Association of Breweriana Advertising Club or the American Breweriana Association if you really want to dive in the hobby.

2. Mantiques from the Prohibition era are clever, but the generation that appreciates its significance has passed on. Collect these items mainly for their historic value.

3. Most beer cans you see on the market are only worth a buck or two so don't drop a lot of cash collecting them. Be picky and buy for sentimental reasons: Cans that remind you of your hometown, your first beer, or the brews Granddad grabbed.

4. Advertising items are great and appeal to a broad range of collectors, hence their ability to hold their value longer than other items.

5. Consider collecting items that spark a conversation. Odd posters, risqué bottle openers, or even neat lamps are awesome and easy to find.

A killer, classic Budweiser Beer die-cut trade sign ad illustration by Andrew Loomis (American, 1892-1959) circa 1930s, from the Estate of Charles Martignette. It sold for $7,767 at auction.

A zeppelin- or dirigible-shaped cocktail shaker with nickel-plated exterior and gold-plated interior. The nose unscrews to expose cover over strainer/juicer opening to flask, base opens to four graduated measures and funnel, and four spoons are stored in the gondola-form compartment. It is 12-1/4" h and sold for $2,000 at auction.

Happy Hour

Tray with black geometric design, chrome frame and handles, dates to the 1930s and is 17-1/4" x 10-1/8". It sold for $687 at auction.

Demand for mantique and vintage whiskey is growing. It's an expensive hobby, but auction houses are working to bring collectible brands to a mainstream market. Shown here from left: a bottle of 1830 Grande Fine Champagne Cognac by Richard & Pailloud (high shoulder, stained label) valued between $1,300 to $1,600; a bottle of 1946 Locke's Kilbeggan Single Irish Whiskey (aged 34 years) valued between $600 and $750; a bottle of 1945 Yellow Chartreuse Taragonne valued at approximately $2,000; a bottle of 1938 Linkwood Pure Highland Malt Whisky by John MacEwan & Co. (aged 44 years) valued at $900 to $1,000; and a circa 1900 bottle of an old cognac fine champagne called MOYET valued at about $600.

The passage of the 18th Amendment to the U.S. Constitution in 1919 prohibited the manufacture, sale, import, or export of intoxicating liquors. Prohibition, as it came to be known, caused more deaths, crime, and corruption than the drink ever did. The amendment was repealed in 1933 by the 21st amendment. This anti-Prohibition figural flask stands 4-3/4" h and sold for $10 at auction.

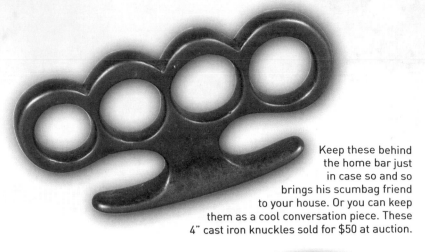

Keep these behind the home bar just in case so and so brings his scumbag friend to your house. Or you can keep them as a cool conversation piece. These 4" cast iron knuckles sold for $50 at auction.

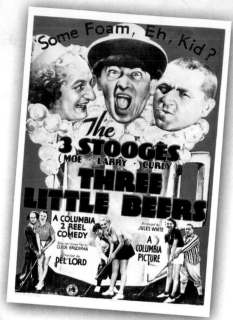

Did you know Dr. Seuss lent his talent to selling brewskies? This tin litho serving tray has bold and colorful Seuss art of "Chief Gansett," the Indian mascot for Narragansett Beer. The 1940s tray is 12" dia. and sold for $385 at auction.

Three Stooges aficionados consider "Three Little Beers" one of the group's best shorts and it's also one of their earliest. One-sheet posters for this 1935 classic from Columbia Pictures are hard to find and this version set a world record for a Three Stooges poster when it sold at auction for $59,750.

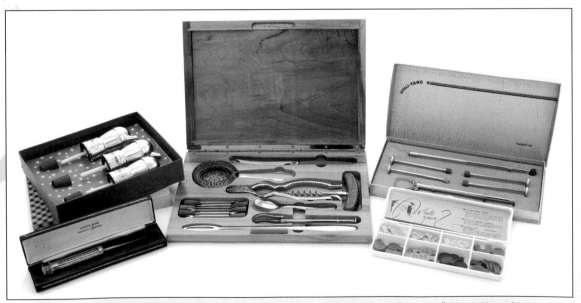

Dating from the late 1930s, this set includes a Gorham silver martini spike, a Bakelite "What's Yours?" drink tag set, a chrome and Bakelite Utili-Tong set, a Mr. Bartender silvered metal gin, vodka, and bourbon pourer, and a German Wusthof stainless and wooded bar tool set with original wooden fitted case. It sold for $34 at auction.

This "Stop for Stag" Stag Beer advertisement by Bill Gregg (American, 20th Century) measures 13-1/4" x 31" and is from the estate of Charles Martignette. It sold for $1,750 at auction.

This cocktail pick holder has chromed mounts and six metal cocktail picks with Bakelite bottle-form ends, 5-1/2" h, $220.

Cocktail pick holder made in France in the early 1930s, 4-3/4" h, $406.

A set of four blonde wood, gray leather upholstered, and chrome-plated metal cocktail bar stools inlaid with glass "Raisins" panels, circa 1990s, 35", sold for $1,792 at auction.

Before the advent of the sports bar and crummy microwave chicken wings, tavern patrons tried their skill on interesting punchboard lottery games. This punchboard features a paste-over image of a bare-breasted pin up girl painted by Gil Elvgren. The board dates to 1950, consists of 1,000 holes to be punched, and is 11-1/4" x 17". It sold for $145 at auction.

This stainless steel cocktail shaker was made by the John Oster Mfg. Co. of Racine, Wis., circa 1940. It stands 16-1/4" h, $150.

You're looking at one of the most expensive beer cans to ever sell at auction. This can for Apache Export Beer has a near perfect body and is likely the best example known to exist. It sold for $24,000.

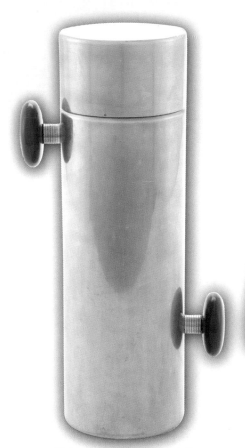

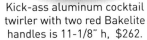

Kick-ass aluminum cocktail twirler with two red Bakelite handles is 11-1/8" h, $262.

Your home bar could have a few generic neon signs. That's easy and will look okay. Not too distinctive, though. So what will set your space apart from any other? This framed World War II nose art removed from a Vickers-Armstrong Mk X Wellington bomber should do the trick. Original nose art from WWII is certainly rare, but rarer still are surviving Royal Australian Air Force examples, mainly because the practice was not as widely adopted by the British and Commonwealth air forces during the war. The Americans had it down pat. The artwork depicts "Father William," the Younger Brewery mascot, pint of beer held high, with "YOUNG/ERS" painted in yellow above and with 19 frothy mugs of beer below. The clever use of mugs of beer to indicate missions is, if not unique, certainly an amusing tribute to the crew's love of the Scottish brand. The art sold for $2,151 at auction.

Cocktail Hour, Al Schmidt (American, 20th Century), watercolor on board, 15" x 12". From the estate of Charles Martignette, it sold at auction for $896.

Men have been admiring Bud girls for more than a century. The first Budweiser girl was introduced in 1883 and she maintained her looks and attire until 1907. The lithograph featured here is from 1904. The Bud girl would no doubt blaze the trail for the bikini-clad Budweiser girls we see at every Super Bowl. This fantastic piece of breweriana measures 24" w x 39-1/4" h overall and sold for $2,151 at auction.

Pin-Up with a Cocktail, Earl Moran (American, 1893-1984), pastel on paper, 20" x 15", $3,346.

CHAPTER
2

FREAKIN' COOL

CURIOSITIES AND ODDITIES

Benny Jack Hinkle III doesn't mind sleeping with a human skeleton hanging in the house. Neither does his 12-year-old son. In fact, as a single father, Benny is in the running for Single Dad of the Year. The two have transformed a 1,000-square-foot apartment into a curiosity cabinet based on the 15th century chambers dedicated to knowledge, enlightenment, and fascination with the natural world.

"This isn't Rooms to Go," Benny says. "I'm drawn to the old gentlemen look, combined with a little creepy. If something catches my eye ... "

Admittedly, a lot of weird and creepy stuff catches Benny's eye. Now 31, Benny's been collecting since he was 16 and still has many of the first pieces of Colonial revival furniture and natural history oddities he picked up years ago.

He was raised by his grandparents whose home was filled with Victorian furniture and interesting old things. His ability to connect with an older generation gave him access to wisdom and opportunities he wouldn't otherwise experience: When he was 16, he walked into an antiques mall and asked the owner if she'd give him a job if he proved to her he was worth the investment. After a day spent moving furniture from one end of the shop to another, he had his first real job and regular access to the odd items that fed his imagination. His apartment is bursting with advertising, tobacciana, taxidermy, and a Victorian-era human skeleton in his computer room.

OPPOSITE PAGE: With this two-headed canary, you get two songs for the price of one. The contemporary smoking sculpture is titled, "The Cuban," and can be found online for about $250.

Benny Jack Hinkle III has always found himself fascinated by the offbeat and unusual. He's transformed his and his son's 1,000-square-foot apartment into a curiosity cabinet—a place devoted to knowledge and an appreciation of the unknown. Even his son has found items for the collection.

You won't see this remote caddy in SkyMall. The taxidermied alligator head isn't something you want to reach into when the lights are too low.

An unknown artist's found object sculpture depicting a mankind's transformation into "cybernetic organisms" is pretty freaking cool.

The apartment's dining area has been converted into an old English pub, complete with a red leather bench and portraits of distinguished gentlemen. The living room is a smoking room for his cigars and a place to watch television, which is cleverly hidden inside a vintage dye cabinet that's been retrofitted to hold a large flat screen. His favorite cigars are Cuba's Montecristo.

Religious icons and paintings from shuttered churches decorate the walls around his desk near his iMac. "Religion has employed a lot of great artists over the years," he says. "That's about as far as I get into it. It's hard for me

MANTIQUES FACT

Curiosity cabinets are encyclopedic collections that are as unique as the collectors who curate them. By their very nature, the boundaries and limits of a curiosity collection are undefined. First documented in the 1600s (but certainly older than that), the curiosity cabinets of the Renaissance served as the cornerstone of the first natural history museums.

The brass chandelier in the office area displays turn-of-the-last-century glass magic lantern slides for a quick biology lesson.

to buy new art. It really has to be something special or something I always wanted to own."

He's encouraged his son, Benny Jack Hinkle IV, to collect as well. The two hit flea markets and he makes it a point to shop at spots that appeal to his son's interests. His room has made space for a few cabinets of his own. One holds collectible farm animals displayed in a vintage hotel key cupboard and another cabinet holds an iguana. His bedroom is ground zero for epic sessions of *Call of Duty*.

True to traditional curiosity cabinets, the entire collection numbers

Benny's Edwardian secretary is home to his iMac and also displays a pair of papier-mâché parade masks and rams, which are shedding their pelts to reveal an unsettling sculpture. The painting in the center was badly damaged, so Benny added his own macabre touchups.

into the thousands of pieces. It has become a way of life. Benny Sr. would rather paint, read, or research his discoveries than watch cable. The unique items stick around but the rest could be gone in a moment.

"If I get tired of a piece, I'll sell it," Benny says. "What I'm looking for is something I've never seen before."

WHERE TO LEARN MORE

⚙ *Cabinets of Wonder* (Abrams, 2012) by Christine Davenne and Christine Fleurent. A comprehensive look at the concept of cabinets of wonder, a centuries-old tradition developed in Europe during the Renaissance. The book shows how a modern-day revival of the curiosity cabinet is taking place in how people collect, decorate homes and restaurants and what it means about our past and future.

⚙ *Cabinet Magazine* (cabinetmagazine.org). *Cabinet* fosters a curiosity about the world by examining an expansive and inclusive definition of culture. The editorial team also publishes books and CDs and organizes exhibitions.

⚙ Museum of Jurassic Technology, 9341 Venice Boulevard, Culver City, California 90232. This museum holds a unique collection of relics and curiosities that harken back to the earliest museums. The exhibits are formally part of other less well-known collections such as microminiatures and micromosaics to "hypersymbolic cognition." It's open Thursday through Sunday and may be found online at mjt.org.

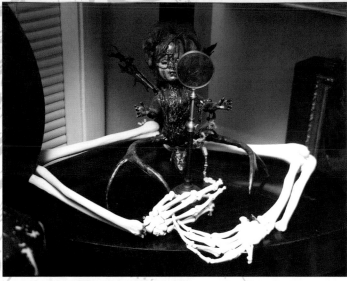

A found-object sculpture of a demon-like creature is enveloped by a pair of human anatomical skeletal models.

A carved 19th century artists' dummy (possibly French) is valued at $1,000. He makes his home next to a candlestick fashioned from a taxidermy turkey leg.

One of Benny's favorite finds is this humidor that opens automatically to present a number of cigars. It's on display with a selection of smoking-themed majolica, such as match and pipe holders.

$460

Wow. I would seriously choke a goat to own something this cool. This 19th century stylized bust is fashioned from mollusk and snail shells by a German company called Korallenästchen, 10" h, $460.

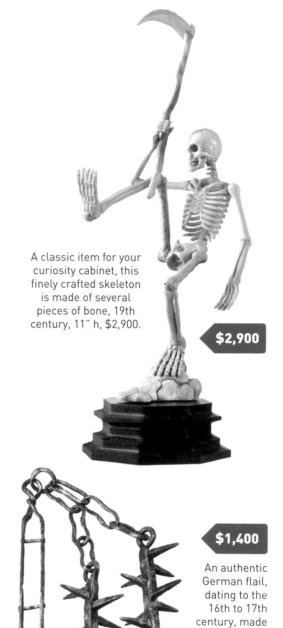

A classic item for your curiosity cabinet, this finely crafted skeleton is made of several pieces of bone, 19th century, 11" h, $2,900.

$2,900

$1,400

An authentic German flail, dating to the 16th to 17th century, made of wrought iron, 27" l, $1,400.

$597

Similar to the one in Benny's collection, this miniature wood and metal guillotine is actually a rare example of prisoner's art from Devil's Island, the infamous French prison off the northern coast of South America. An inscription under the lid of the coffin, which lies beside the machine of death, reads, "Ile du Diable / H de H 1928." An accompanying handwritten letter from legendary collector Robert White asserts that it was purchased years ago from a doctor's collection of prison art. Devil's Island was abandoned in 1938. This highly detailed model is in excellent condition and stands 14" h, $597.

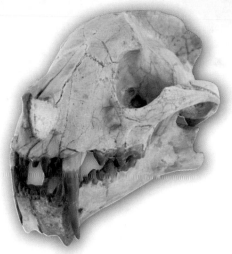

Fossilized skull of a Dinictis squalidens, aka, a sabre-toothed cat. These amazing creatures first appeared in the fossil record 34-38 million years ago and their well-developed canine teeth were specialized to deliver a powerful blow that likely severed the jugular or sliced through the windpipe of its prey. Measuring 4-1/2" w, 7" l, 3-3/4" h, the skull sold at auction for $3,635.

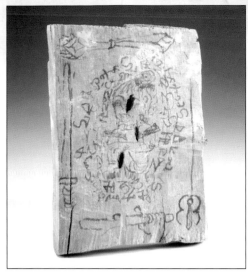

This wood board dates to the 5th or 6th century A.D. and is inscribed with a curse used during an Aghori ritual practice known as kilana. Once performed in an ancient area of India, the practice involved pulverized human bones. It measures 8-1/4" h x 5-1/2" w and sold for $657.

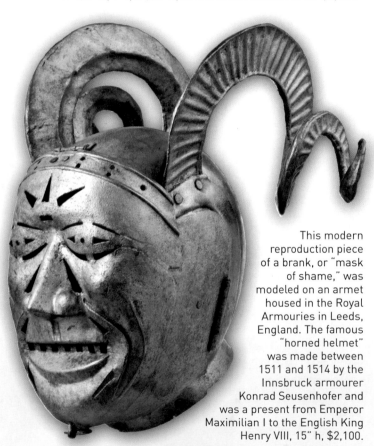

This modern reproduction piece of a brank, or "mask of shame," was modeled on an armet housed in the Royal Armouries in Leeds, England. The famous "horned helmet" was made between 1511 and 1514 by the Innsbruck armourer Konrad Seusenhofer and was a present from Emperor Maximilian I to the English King Henry VIII, 15" h, $2,100.

This extremely rare Ojibwa shaman's ritual suit and material dates to the 1880s and includes a hand drum, several rattles, pipes, charms, herbal medicines, and weasel skins. The set sold at auction for $21,900.

"Bone of a horse / killed at Custer battle with Sitting Bull / June 25, 1876." It's believed the bone came from a reburial in 1877 or 1879 of the bones still left at the scene of Custer's massacre, and is 11-1/4" l. Artifacts like this are often found at auction for $3,000-$5,000.

This stack of books makes it easy to study as it hides a 20th century French Baccarat decanter. Measuring 8-3/4" x 11-1/2" x 8-1/4", $4,867.

A wicked cool French art deco and bronze floor lamp in the form of a cobra emerging from a basket, circa 1920, by Edgar Brandt (French, 1880-1960), 58-5/8" h, $4,687.

A unique 19th century English rosewood humidor table is actually telescoping and made of a drum table with top that lifts vertically to reveal fitted compartments for cigars and accessories. It measures 40-1/2" h x 20" w, open, $2,000.

Pair of onyx table lamps with pyramidal shades, 20th c, 24-1/2" h, valued between $1,500 to $2,500.

This circa 1900 Gothic revival cabinet has two vertical doors above a single door opening to shelves, and carved panels with figures, 73-5/8" h x 45-3/4" w x 19-1/4" d, $5,975.

The next time you see a cabinet like this, feel free to shout: "Hey, what a great contador!" A contador is a cabinet with multiple drawers that's set on a stand. This Indi-Portuguese teak contador dates to the late 19th and early 20th century and measures 26" h x 27" w x 16-1/2" d, $875.

Great early 20th century English leather library chair measures 40" h x 32-1/2" d and is valued between $600 to $900.

This oil on canvas is *Judith with the Head of Holofernes*. In the eponymous Book of Judith, she is a widow who proved her devotion to her late husband by fake-seducing enemy General Holofernes until he let her into his tent one night while he was drunk. Then the beheading. Bolognese School (17th century), 31-1/4" x 46", $1,250.

Yeah, these are plaster casts of human feet; don't expect a lot of company. From the 20th century and 15" h, $750.

A box of spells: The removable drawer has compartments including several partially silver-set amulets and two paper slips with devotional images that are meant to be swallowed. Among the items: a skull carved out of bone with the motto, "AIEAOU" - a symbolic device used by the Europe's Habsburg emperors - a St. Paul's tongue (fossilized shark tooth); viper vertebrae; various pendants of semi-precious stone and two paper slips with conjuring spells, 23" x 16" x 9-1/2", $2,900.

This authentic 17th century riveted chastity belt puts the anus in tetanus. If the lock doesn't stop you, the jagged edges will. Dating to the 17th century, it's 12" w and sold at auction for $1,100.

A rostrum - or snout - of the Common swordfish (Pristis pristis), 20th century, 60 completely preserved teeth, 46" l, can be found at auction for about $3,000 to $5,000.

A collection of butterflies in a Riker specimen mount sold at auction for $2,031.

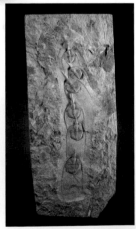

This unusual fossil looks like six Ampyx Trilobites marching in a "conga line," but this linear procession is the result of the critters being aligned in a channel drift in the ancient Draa Valley of Morocco. It measures 11" h x 4-3/4" w x 3/4" d and sold at auction for $2,062.

Stunning branch of red precious coral with multiple twigs mounted on a heavy pyrite cube, with a profiled wooden base, 12" h, $3,070.

Interesting branch of red precious coral and large branch of soft coral with opalised ammonites and pearls mounted on a green marbled base, 14" h, $1,070.

It's not unreasonable to think that stones were the first objects human collected. This set of artifact stones includes an East Indian Stone Lingam, a large oval sacred stone with stand measuring 4-1/4" w x 7-1/4" h, a pre-historic smooth stone axe head, 6-3/4" l, and a small pre-historic smooth stone scraping tool, 6-1/2" l The set is valued between $200 to $300.

Perfect for your late night smokes, this collection of 41 cigarette holders spans the late 19th and early 20th century and are made of amber or meerschaum or with gold and silver mounts, $812.

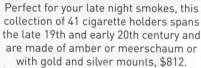

Few people can say they own a 50-year-old olive, but this clear glass display jar has that and more. This was a marketing tool for Heinz Pickling Vinegar used to store homemade products for table use. It is 19" h and sold at auction for $430.

This fantastic group of 19th century surgical tools includes a Tenaculum, or chained hooks used for pulling out the arteries from the limb stump in order to tie them off, surgical needles, a Hey's Saw used in a trephine operation to reduce fractures of bones of the skull, a bone spoon (how nasty is that?!), a nickel-plated oval brass snuff box engraved with a Schooner, a brass oval tinder box, an oval tin snuff box with chain attached, and an octagonal tin snuff box. The entire set sold for just $47.

Twelve terrorists. One cop.
The odds are against John McClane…
That's just the way he likes it.

BRUCE WILLIS
DIE HARD

TWENTIETH CENTURY FOX Presents A GORDON COMPANY/SILVER PICTURES Production A JOHN McTIERNAN Film BRUCE WILLIS DIE HARD
ALAN RICKMAN ALEXANDER GODUNOV BONNIE BEDELIA Music by MICHAEL KAMEN Visual Effects Produced by RICHARD EDLUND Film Editors FRANK J. URIOSTE, A.C.E.
and JOHN F. LINK Production Designer JACKSON DeGOVIA Director of Photography JAN De BONT Executive Producer CHARLES GORDON Screenplay By JEB STUART and STEVEN E. de SOUZA
Based on the novel by RODERICK THORP Produced by LAWRENCE GORDON and JOEL SILVER Directed by JOHN McTIERNAN Read The Fawcett Paperback.
Color by DeLuxe

COMING THIS JULY

Printed in the U.S.A.

Hands down, my favorite action movie. *Die Hard* is
like a living super hero flick on steroids. This 1988
poster sells for about $100 at auction.

STAR POWER

ENTERTAINMENT MEMORABILIA

So you're planning your home theater and after all the cords are hidden and your Chromecast is plugged in, and your Bluetooth speakers are hung, you still have to fill 99 percent of the walls.

What are you gonna do? You're going to turn to the Interwebs and find some cool, one-of-a-kind conversation pieces that set your movie room apart of all the others on your block. It doesn't take a lot of cash to build a solid collection. Try focusing your efforts on a specific genre, such as science fiction or Westerns. You'll be shocked at how much cool you can get for a few hundred bucks.

You can start with posters from your favorite movies. Doesn't matter how obscure they are. Movie posters make a space. Then branch out to movie props, animation cels, or even costumes. Auction houses and various online sellers have made it efficient for you to own a piece of Hollywood. It is cool seeing a film or a television episode and spot one of the items you have in your mantiques collection.

If you're on a slimmer budget, consider signed black and white promotional photographs of your favorite stars. You can find them in online auctions for a few bucks. Check out Premier Props, Heritage Auctions, and Profiles in History for fast sources of cool stuff. All three hold regular sales of new and vintage props. You'll have the coolest home theater this side of Coruscant.

The scarf John Wayne wore in the title role in *Rooster Cogburn*, the 1973 sequel to *True Grit*, has so much testosterone in it that I'm shocked it hasn't fathered a child or been arrested in a bar fight. This scarf is manlier than you. Face it. It sold for $4,182 at auction.

Deck the walls with the shirt Elvis Presley wore in the 1968 western *Charro*. The shirt was displayed in the Elvis-A-Rama Museum for many years. It sold for $6,250.

This Andy Warhol limited edition print, titled "John Wayne," is numbered and signed in pencil in the lower right hand corner, "221/250 Andy Warhol." A number of years after Wayne's death, Warhol used this image (a publicity still from *The Man Who Shot Liberty Valance*) without permission. To resolve this situation, the Warhol Foundation gifted this print to Wayne's family. It measures 36" x 36" and sold for $77,675 at auction.

This here is a hubcap from Elvis' prized 1973 Lincoln Continental six-door limousine that he gave to J. D. Sumner. Framed to an overall size of 24" x 24", it brought $956 at auction.

This shadow box display featuring the late Heath Ledger as The Joker has three playing cards, a prop Batarang, two realistic looking US Peace Silver Dollars (one clean, the other blackened), and an "I Believe in Harvey Dent" 3" pinback button as seen in the film. It sold for just $125.

Some people don't trust people who don't drink alcohol or coffee ... I don't trust anyone who doesn't love *The Shawshank Redemption*. The poster for this 1994 Columbia classic sold for $597 at auction.

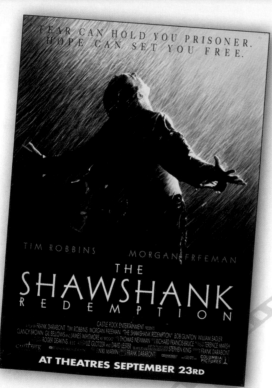

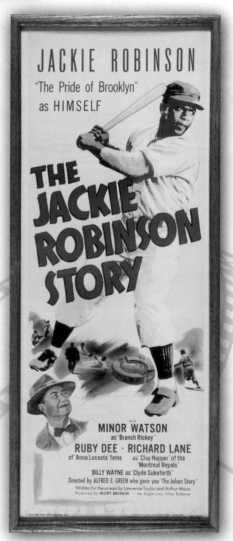

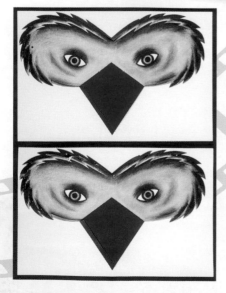

In 1963, the person wearing these masks would be admitted to a free showing of Alfred Hitchcock's *The Birds* if the number matching their mask was pulled from a drum. As if the movie was freaky enough, imagine a bunch of little kids scurrying around your feet like mutant pigeons. They measure 6" x 9" and sold for $262 at auction.

Yet another important step in the integration of baseball came in 1950 when a film celebrating the arrival of the Major Leagues' first African-American player hit the silver screen. This 14" x 36" insert format poster was issued to cinemas screening the picture. It sold for $657 at auction.

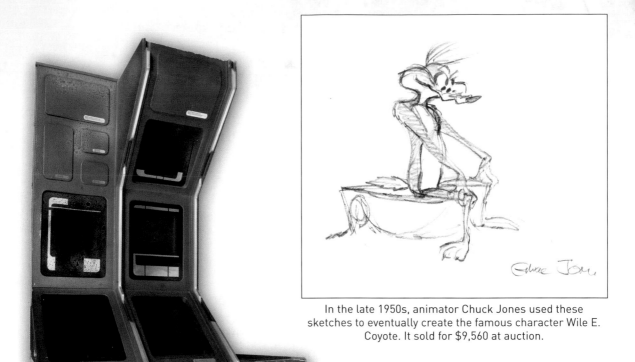

In the late 1950s, animator Chuck Jones used these sketches to eventually create the famous character Wile E. Coyote. It sold for $9,560 at auction.

This large workstation/console was used in sets seen in episodes of the *Star Trek: Voyager* television series. The set fixture was seen in the Science Labs in the Season 5 episode "Drone" and was also part of the main engineering set in the final season of the series. It sold for $358 at auction.

What could finish off your home theater better than this art deco number? This Kodascope, Model B, was made by the Eastman Kodak Company of Rochester, New York, circa 1930. The burl walnut skyscraper storage case with ebonized lattice pattern opens to reveal a Kodascope 16 mm film projector. It sold for $1,500 at auction.

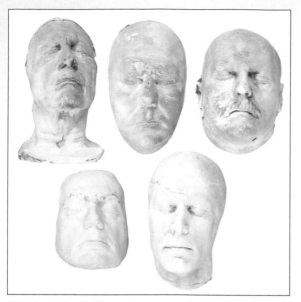

This is a thing? Where else can you hang a collection of five plaster life masks of cast members of the classic NBC sitcom *Cheers*, including Ted Danson, George Wendt, Rhea Perlman, John Ratzenberger, and Kelsey Grammer. These lifecasts were made by taking a mold of each actor's face using alginate, a fragile but accurate casting material made from seaweed. The set sold at auction for $298.

This hand-inked, hand-painted animation production cel is from the final scene of the 1934 short, *Let's You and Him Fight*, featuring a victorious Popeye and a defeated Bluto in the ring. It sold for $8,365 at auction.

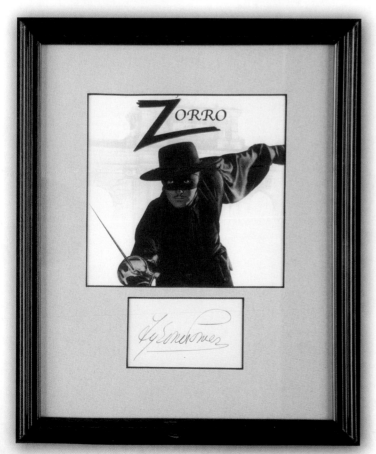

Smooth criminal: This framed and autographed lithograph image of Tyrone Power is 8" x 10" and sold for $448 at auction.

This rare 1909 motiograph silent film hand-cranked theater projector consists of two large reel housings, lens, electrified light housing, slide bar, and the three original adjustable knobs that control the intensity of the light source. It sold for $3,585 at auction.

The interesting story behind the monster shown on the poster for the 1957 film *Voodoo Woman* is that it had already made an appearance in a movie a year earlier. Creature creator Paul Blaisdell grabbed the costume he'd made for *The She Creature*, ripped off the tail, fins, and pincer claws, then took the cracked stone scale body that was left, wrapped it in burlap, and topped it with a skull mask and a big blond wig. No 1950s movie poster collection is complete without a matched pair of the 1956 *The She Creature* and *Voodoo Woman* one sheets framed side by side. The poster art is by legendary artist Albert Kallis. This *Voodoo Woman* poster sold for $239 at auction, and *The She Creature* for $836.

This French stone lithograph theater poster featuring *La Yetta*, a belly dancer, was printed by F. Garric, Paris, circa 1900. The 61" poster sold for $690 at auction.

Theater District, watercolor painting by Harry Walker (American, mid 20th century) showing a 1930s scene of a city theater district with brightly lit marquees in a nighttime setting. Painted in 1978, the work sold for $230 at auction.

So if you're picking out furniture for your man cave or home theater, are you going to prowl the aisles of a sanitized Ikea or are you going to buy this 8-foot couch custom-made for Glenn Ford for the personal bar in his house? I thought so.

This couch has seen more celebrity ass than Groucho Marx's whoopee cushion. In fact, it's the very spot Ford bedded Marilyn Monroe. The couch is also accompanied by a haunting painting of a little girl that Ford had given Monroe, which was her favorite. On the reverse of the painting, Ford provided a detailed, handwritten account of his time with Marilyn, including a romantic encounter on the aforementioned couch. He writes in part:

"This was Marilyn Monroe's favorite painting - after she had been through the house ... Her psychiatrist had made her cry. She said, 'Glenn take me home.' We got in my car and I did not know where she lived. She said, 'No Glenn, your home' - where she stayed all night in the bar on the plaid sofa. She said, 'Just hold me' and I did - and more. I still have this because she forgot it." Ford also adds: "I think Marilyn wanted to die. When we made love, she whispered, 'I wish I could die right now, while I'm happy.' " It sold for $4,780 at auction.

This serial poster for *Flash Gordon's Trip to Mars* (Universal International) dates to the late 1940s and measures 27" x 41". It sold for $663.

Boasting graphics that are far superior to many of the American-made posters, this British quad, spanning an impressive 30" x 40", is full of scenes that made *From Russia with Love* a huge James Bond hit; $5,676.

A little something to hang between your boards, Laguna Beach artist Tom Belloni's 10' x 4' painting of a single short board surfer completing a beautiful cutback to the top of a wave was completed in the late 1970s. It's valued at $1,000 to $3,000.

CHAPTER 4

CALIFORNIA GOLD

SURFING COLLECTIBLES

Belloni '77

A vacation in your house. That's what vintage surfing collectibles are. Doesn't matter if it's snowing out. Hell no. Every time you gaze at your vintage board or flip through a scarce book on the sport, you're instantly back. Sun. Salt water. Sweat. Beautiful bodies. Heaven.

The market for vintage surf stuff is just now coming into its own. Dealers say they are moving thousands of vintage shirts a year—some with prices in the four digits. A couple of grand for a shirt? If it's a rare and classic Hawaii Calls pattern made by Kilohana then you can easily expect to shell out nearly $3,000—the value of two Armani suits. These Rayon wonders have hit a stride and to build a decent collection, you can expect to spend between $100 to $250 per shirt.

Surprisingly, that amount can also get you started in vintage surfboards. There are a few auction houses and many more dealers who trade in vintage boards. Like most other mantiques, the older and scarcer the board, the more you can expect to pay for a primo specimen. There are tales of California collectors getting steals on vintage boards from Hawaii, but they are constantly on the hunt.

Hawaii's Surfing Heritage & Culture Center holds a fundraising auction every year and organizers always seem to find some excellent examples or rare boards. We're talking boards that are approaching 90 years old and prices that move as high as a honker and as fast as cruncher.

The year 1969 was epic for surf along the California coast and nobody took better advantage of all that swell than Santa Barbara's master shaper Reynolds Yater. While other shapers radically expanded and contracted their templates, Yater's subtle style crafted some of the cleanest, most highly functional surfboards of the period, including this 7' 6" Pocket Rocket at right. It sold at auction for $2,300.

This 1979 design by Esteban Bojorquez aka Steve Krajewski and built by Greg Liddle Surfboards combines color, humor, and texture. For over a decade with the Liddle shop, Krajewski designed and rode several low buoyancy, parallel rail speed machines. This one is 6' 9" and sold at auction for $3,300

One of the most sought-after surfboards to exist, this 1949 Pete Peterson model is not only one of the rarest boards in existence, it's also the most remarkable. Peterson remains the greatest California waterman of the first half of the 20th century, winning the West Coast Championships four times ('32, '36, '38 and '41). He was also one of the sport's most innovative designers. The board is a hollow balsa/plywood composite and an amazing slice of surf culture. It sold at auction for $32,400.

The Hobie Bi-Sect at left was designed as the ultimate travel board, ostensibly for use during the production of Bruce Brown's documentary epic *The Endless Summer*. The Bi-Sect featured an innovative joint apparatus that allowed the board to be segmented into two pieces. Very few were actually made and even less survived the decades and this model has a fully functioning center joint, matching joint and stringer detailing, glass tailblock, and glasson fin. It sold at auction for $6,750.

For a short time in the 1970s, Hobie surfboards introduced a board logo called "Positive Force" that was created by surf artist Bill Ogden. This board retains one of these original Hobie "Positive Force" logos, is 6' 6", and valued at $100-$150.

This 1963 Bing "showcase" longboard features a unique design element that was not easy to perfect. It is decorated by inlaying contrasting wood in a double "figure 8" pattern crossing each other on both the top and bottom of the foam blank (rather than just routed into the deck). The inlay is comprised of a balsa, redwood. The entire board measures 9' 4" and is valued at $1,000 to $3,000.

Only one collectible surfboard has ever inspired an actual counterfeiting ring and this genuine, original 1966 Greg Noll 'Da Cat at right is one of the most famous—and infamous— surfboard model of the 1960s. 'Da Cat was named for legendary Malibu surfer and cultural provocateur Mickey Dora. They were counterfeited, but this particular board, with its blue pigment panels, original stickers, and glass-on Dora speed fin, is one of 'Da Cat's earlier incarnations and is in excellent condition. Strangely, some counterfeits are worth more than the originals. It sold for $8,000 at auction.

Boards shaped by legendary California proto-stylist Matt Kivlin are a collector's dream and this 1949 balsa "Chip," at left, is no exception. Kivlin returned from his first Hawaii surf trip in 1947 influenced by the superior surfing of "Rabbit" Kekai and others. Soon Kivlin was modifying boards to be thinner, narrower, and lighter, using lightweight balsawood covered with fiberglass, called "chips." This board was found in Idaho and was reglassed by Jim Phillips before it sold for $31,000 at auction.

Few boards survive from the 1930s and this unrestored one is a museum's centerpiece. This unique redwood plank is made from just two redwood pieces glued together. It sports an unusual rounded tail, found on only a few wood boards from this era, indicating that its unknown shaper was willing to experiment with new design elements back in the mid-1930s. It's 8' 8" and sold for $7,000 at auction.

The Weber Performer is a classic 1960s longboard and is perhaps the most popular surfboard model ever produced. Shaped in early 1967 (check out the hip paisley print nose inlay) this monster is 9-plus feet and represents the last commercial run of longboards to be made before the late 1967 "Shortboard Revolution" rendered it obsolete. It sold at auction for $6,500.

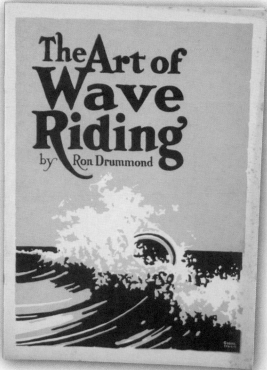

This copy of *The Art of Wave Riding* by Ronald Blake "Canoe" Drummond (1907-1996) comes direct from the Drummond family. A 1931 first edition of just 500 copies printed, the book is eagerly sought by collectors. Drummond's primer is seen as the very first surfing publication ever and this remarkably preserved copy sold for $1,700 at auction.

No, They Are Not Hawaiian Shirts

Here's a great way to instantly become 35 percent cooler than a lot of other guys. Mantiques collectors know that the rayon works of art you see here are not called "Hawaiian shirts." Oh no. The correct term is "Aloha Shirt."

The vintage Aloha Shirt is a celebration of the charm from the golden age of Old Hawaii (1930-1950). The value of a vintage Aloha Shirt depends on the material, the condition, rarity, size, and manufacturer. Collectors favor shirts with words that read like advertisements for Hawaii or those that come in bright colors such as red and yellow. If you want to collect to someday resell, stick with iconic images of surfing, pineapples, ukuleles, birds, fish, rainbows, amazing flowers, canoeing, tikis, paddling, sailing, and popular tourist attractions like luaus, Aloha Tower, Diamond Head, hula shows, and the King Kamehameha statue. Hunt down shirts made by the four oldest companies that made the originals: Aloha (Ellery Chun King-Smith), Kahala, Kamehameha, and Musashiya.

Other key makers of original vintage Aloha Shirts include: Alii Lole, Aloha King-Smith, Andrade, Artvogue, Ashfield, Campus, Catalina, Diamondhead Sportswear, Duke Kahanamoku, Hale Hawaii, Hawaiian Surf, HoAloha, Hookano, Iolani, Jantzen, Kahala, Kamehameha, Kilohana, Kramer's, Kuonakakai, Lauhala, Liberty House, Made in California, Made in Hawaii, Malihini, McGregor, McInerny's, Musashiya, Nani, Okolehao, Pali, Paradise Sportswear, Penneys, Pilgrim, Polynesian Sportswear, Ross Sutherland, Royal Hawaiian, Shaheen's, Surfriders Sportswear, and Waikiki Sports.

Long-sleeved Aloha Shirts were originally designed for the winter months in Hawaii or formal occasions.

MANTIQUES FACTS

Collectors prefer "silkies"—old rayon shirts that have a silky feel. Because of their demand, silky rayon shirts usually have the highest value; however, the earliest Aloha Shirts from the 1930s actually were made from real silk.

In old Hawaii, surfing was the sport of royalty. One can at least look like a King in this late 1950s shirt called the "Big Wave" print. The style is called a border print and, like all other Aloha Shirts, is not meant to be tucked in. The red version of this shirt was one of the five Aloha shirts that were made into postage stamps by the U.S. Postal Service issued on June 2, 2012. The blue version is the most appropriate due to the realistic ocean colors, but this shirt was also printed in red and brown versions. It is made from cotton by Malihini (meaning newcomer) and is valued between $300 and $500.

This early 1940s rayon Kamehameha find is prized for its black background, deemed by many collectors as the most valuable because it can match anything from a pair of old Levis to modern-day khakis. The selvage (finished edges of fabric) on the inside by the buttonholes of many early original Kamehameha shirts have the words "Kamehameha Prints" sewn inside. It is valued between $2,800 and $3,200.

RULES FOR WEARING A VINTAGE ALOHA SHIRT

1. Never tuck it in.

2. Pants - all pants match every Aloha Shirt.

3. Resist the urge to wear black socks with sandals. This is really just a good life lesson.

4. Rum in a hollow pineapple is optional.

This is an especially rare "cabana set" made by Kamehameha in the 1940s – the trunks are usually damaged from sitting or by pool bleach. The set was made of nylon so it would dry quicker and is valued at between $2,300 and $2,700.

If you're going to invest in one vintage Aloha Shirt, this is it: The classic "pineapple print" manufactured in the 1940s by Cisco under the name of the legendary surfer Duke Kahanamoku. Hawaiian native Kahanamoku won gold and silver Olympic medals in the early 1900s for swimming and was known as Hawaii's "Ambassador of Aloha" until his death in 1968. This pineapple print comes in a variety of background colors including blue, red, white, black, green, and brown. It is made of silky rayon and valued between $800 and $1,000.

"Back panel" or "back print" design Aloha Shirts are valued by high-end collectors, especially in Japan and the Middle East, because some of the images on the shirts have risqué poses of women, which are taboo in some cultures. This 1940s shirt was made by Catalina from a thicker type of rayon commonly referred to as "sharkskin" and is valued between $1,300 and $1,700.

This vertical print was made by HoAloha (meaning friend). The HoAloha label was used on some Sears, Roebuck and Co. Hawaiian apparel from 1958-1960. This cotton marvel is valued between $300 and $400.

Used Cars "Safety
Tested" Oldsmobile sign,
42" diameter, $4,250.

CHAPTER 5

SWEET WHEELS

THE VINTAGE GARAGE

Gil's first car was a 1955 Chevy Bel Aire—a rare Navajo tan and India ivory classic—and he still gets to look at it every single day. He picked it up in 1975 as a high school student for about $225, but now it's a project car that brings back a flood of memories after every hour he spends on it. "If I had the time, it'd be done in a month, but as it is, it's been years."

He's got it parked in his "working garage" right in front of four display cases packed with Corgi, Dinky, and Matchbox finds he's collected over the years. A few represent the more than 100 classic or special vintage cars he's owned and sold during the past 30 years and a few he wishes he could one day own.

For Gil, his collection has served as both a pastime and a way to invest his money to bankroll his hobby and his retirement. Unlike CDs, he knows that a 1972 Mercedes 250c will probably generate a better return than a $5,000 CD at his local bank. Once the '55 Chevy is done, he's got big plans to finally own his own "Rod" and there's already a 1937 LaSalle coupe waiting in the wings. "If it's a screaming deal, I'll buy it," he says.

That's how he came to own one of his favorite cars, and a notable one at that. As a university student, he remembered catching glimpses of a professor's red 1959 Maserati 3500GT Touring Superleggera traveling around town. It wasn't until a few years later that he was back in town to buy a different car that he and that Maserati would cross paths again.

"I was with a buddy and we were in town to buy a Pontiac Grand Prix convertible until the seller changed his mind. So we're disappointed and end up driving around and came across that same red Maserati parked alongside a house," Gil says. "So we knock on the door and talked to the guy and

The collection of motorcycles includes a 1973 BMW R75/5, a 1972 Muto Guzzi Ambassador, and a 1972 Honda CB500 shown here in front of a 1959 Maserati 3500GT Touring Superleggera and below Gil's collection of Schwinn bicycles.

Gil's 1968 Shelby GT500 Mustang, retaining its original factory paint and finish, is one of his favorite riding cars. He takes it to local car shows but has a hard time getting it though fast food drive-thru windows: "Everyone's stopping us, so they can get their picture taken in front of the car."

wouldn't you know that it's the same professor who owned the car back then. I asked him if he wanted to sell it and he said, 'Yeah, sure.' Here we were, with cash, a truck, and a trailer. It all worked out great."

Come to find out, the Maserati was a movie star. It was the very same car Rock Hudson drove in a 1978 television miniseries called "Wheels," a soap opera set in the auto industry complete with corporate spying and power struggles.

"The car is in the show a lot. The story goes they were having trouble with the Maserati engine, so they pulled it and slapped a Chevy engine in. I found an original engine and transmission and it's over there," he says, pointing to a mound covered by a gray shop blanket. For now the Mas, complete with a welded tubular construction, is another project that increases in value every year, whether Gil touches it or not.

The Maserati is parked in his "collection garage" next to a stunningly original 1968 Shelby GT500, which Gil drives to car meets and occasionally to drive-thru diners.

By far the most prized item in the entire collection is this 1966 Jaguar XKE E-Type Series 1 coupe. "It's fun to drive – just a joy," Gil says.

"People come up all the time and ask to get their picture taken with it," he says.

Behind the Shelby is perhaps his favorite car: a 1966 Jaguar XKE E-Type Series 1 coupe. The pride and joy was picked up some years ago and is still a blast to drive. Besides minor tune-ups, he installed an aluminum radiator for the 4.2 liter engine and changed out

In the working garage, Gil keeps the first car he ever owned: a 1955 Chevrolet Bel Aire. The outside is fully prepared and ready for a complete overhaul of the interior.

WHERE TO LEARN MORE

- *Garage Style Magazine*, garagestylemagazine. com. This magazine is 100 percent devoted to garages and collections. Besides vintage autos, it covers collectibles such as automobilia, petroliana, neon and porcelain signs, and even die-cast cars.

- HotWheelscollectors.com. Official site by Mattel on current and past models and collector forums.

- Dinky Toys Collectors Association (dtcawebsite. org). A hub for collectors who plan meetings, magazines, and branch out to even smaller collecting categories of these die-cast miniature vehicles.

the gas tank. "Four-wheel independent suspension and four-wheel disk brakes. This is a keeper, for sure."

The car reminds him of a time before a wave of 1968 safety regulations banned covered headlamps and low bumpers.

Other drivers include a 1969 Austin-Healey Sprite, and a 1949 Hudson Super 6. "I regret selling every cool car I ever owned," Gil says.

Between two rows of cars, Gil stores his riding motorcycles, including a 1973 BMW R75/5, a classy 1972 Muto Guzzi Ambassador, and a 1972 Honda CB500. He also keeps a few fun-to-own cycles like his Yamaha RD400 ("It's a screamer"), a 1976 Honda 750 (ready for a paint job), and a 1958 BSA Golden Flash. "None of my stuff is perfect," Gil says. "I've had perfect before and all you do is sell it."

Overlooking the entire shebang are four walls of manly stuff: Overhead hangs 18 bikes, most of them vintage Schwinn bikes from the late 1950s to the 1960s, a camera collection, a couple of typewriters, and a JBL and Yamaha stereo system capable of really annoying his entire neighborhood. On the day I visited him, the stereo filled the garage with Neil Young's "Unknown Legend," the perfect song for a garage packed with Americana memories and plenty of work to do.

A collection of vintage car emblems and logos hangs in one of two garages holding Gil's extensive auto collection.

Gil's collection of 18 Schwinn bikes spans 20 years of popular makes, including this banana seat wonder from the 1970s.

Gil picked up the majority of his Dinky, Hubley, Corgi, Tootsie Toy, and Matchbox cars and cast iron vehicles during the early years of eBay. "I would just put in my best bid and move on to the next auction. It was great," he says. This bookcase is also home to a small collection of airplane models, an extensive library of car repair manuals, and copies of Arthur Logoz's *AutoParade* from the 1960s.

$69,000

$776

Stunning DuPont-era 1935 Indian Chief motorcycle is one of Steve McQueen's better restorations and was originally sold from McQueen's collection in 1984. It later changed hands at auction for $69,000. Badass fact: McQueen was expelled from the Carnegie Institute of Technology for riding his motorcycle through the College of Fine Arts building.

Steve McQueen was also an avid car aficionado and performed many of his own driving stunts in movies such as *Bullitt* and *The Great Escape*. In this photograph, McQueen poses with car inventor Carroll Shelby by his prototype model Ford Cobra sports car at Shelby's Venice, California plant in 1964. Photo by Lester Nehamkin; $776.

$12,075

Sporting a 500cc, 2-cylinder, engine serial number C-2395, this 1951 Indian Blackhawk Chief motorcycle sold at auction for $12,075.

One of the oldest and most sought after motorcycles by the undisputed king of motorcycles. This 1912 Harley-Davidson Silent Grey Fellow motorcycle is a 5 horsepower, 35-cubic-inch machine driven by a flat leather belt. Weighing in at approximately 195 pounds, this single-speed bike had a top speed of 45 mph. It sold at auction for $27,025.

Awesome and bright 1913 Indian V-Twin motorcycles like these are hard to find. It was made the first year Indian offered both front and rear suspension (a.k.a. "Spring Cradle Frame"). This V-Twin 74-cubic-inch motorbike sold at auction for $16,100.

The story goes that the Russians captured a BMW motorcycle during World War II, copied it for their own use, and used these bikes against the German military, perhaps aiding America's victory in WWII. These can still be found at auction ranging from $5,500 to $6,500.

This 1947 Indian Chief Roadmaster with whitewall tires and 74-cubic-inch engine was restored in the early 1980s by Alabama Classic Motorcycles. It sold at auction for $27,025.

Bus driver's wool hat with Peerless System metal hat badge, $75.

Okay, kinda kooky, but this hand-crafted large-scale life-size wicker Harley-Davidson motorcycle is pretty damn cool. It features dual exhaust, turning front end, brake and clutch cables. It measures 80" l x 45" h and sold at auction for $345.

Quick Change, Brown & Bigelow calendar illustration, Gil Elvgren (American, 1914-1980), 1967, oil on canvas, signed lower right, 30" x 24", $110,500.

Penn Auto Refinishing calendar, 1931, offset and color lithograph of the work of Spanish painter Luis Ricardo Falero (Spanish, 1851-1896), measures 29-1/2" x 17-12". From the estate of Charles Martignette, it sold at auction for $275.

Ou la la ... calendar pin up blotters, 1940s, offered as a 14-piece selection of cards. Calendars date from December 1947 to December 1948 with advertising from various firms. Each item displays a classic image of 1940s cheesecake, mostly from the work of notable artists Earl Moran and Gil Elvgren; $33.

76 Outboard Fuel Gasoline sign, 11-1/2" d, $350.

Beacon Security Gasoline "A Caminol Product" Lighthouse die-cut sign, 48" x 30", $55,000. Rated 9.5 out of 10 for condition, the sign is likely the finest example known to exist. When it sold in early 2013, it set a record and elevated the price ceiling for the entire petroliana advertising sign market. The auction was held by Matthews Auctions, LLC, based in Nokomis, Ill., prior to the Chicagoland Petroliana & Advertising Show in Peotone, Ill.

Atlantic Motorboat Oil "Brand New Power" counter-top display with round quart metal can, $525.

Small Amoco flame sign, lighted plastic, $100.

This BMW convexed sign with classic logo is a rare pre-war piece, 24" in diameter, $2,250.

Rare 1933 Cadillac V8, V12, V16 Lasalle V8
with logos sign, 24" x 30", $33,000.

Cadillac Authorized Service With Crest
Logo, 42" diameter, $3,750.

Certified Garages
Of America
Association &
Authorized Member By
Invitation, $3,700.

Champlin Motor
Oil sign, 42" x
28", $250.

Rare size
Ford Tractor
Ferguson
Systems
Authorized
Dealer
"Wheel-less
Implements"
with logo,
$2,700.

Hard-to-find
Ferrari with
Horse Logo
self-framed
sign, 34" x
18", $8,500.

Ford (mid-size)
oval sign, 23" x
33", $950.

Gilmer Moulder Rubber Fan Belt counter-top metal cabinet display, 22" x 16" x 26", $175.

Golden West Oil Company sign, with Baby Blue Mountains graphics, $2,700.

Greyhound with graphics sign, 24" x 40", $450.

Harbor Petroleum Products double-sided porcelain die-cut sign with sea plane graphics, $8,250.

IGA Grocery store sign with eagle logo, 12" x 13", $200.

Jaguar Sales & Service sign with logo in original hanging frame, 42" x 39", $7,000.

This new old stock (NOS) John Deere two-legged Deer embossed self-framed sign, 42" x 38", $375.

Incredibly rare Authorized Mack Truck Service "Performance Counts" Shovel Nose Style, $9,500.

Mercedes-Benz Service sign with logo, 42" in diameter, $4,000.

Mileage Gasoline with tire in motion logo sign, 14" x 20", $400.

Rare Mobiloil single-sided porcelain shield-shaped sign with both Gargoyle and Pegasus logos, $3,850.

Mohawk Gasoline sign with rare orange background, 15" single lens, $3,200.

Oliver Farm Implements "Plowmakers For The World" sign with logo, 14" x 48", $2,200.

Old Fort Feeds with great graphics, $1,600.

North Dakota Route 28 Highway sign, 15" x 15", $375.

Oldsmobile Service porcelain flange sign, 16" x 22", $900.

Five-pound metal can for Packard Cup Grease by Wolverine Lubricants, $375.

Packard Universal Joint Graphite Grease Twenty-five Pound Round Bucket, $200.

This original and hard-to-find Porsche Stuttgart sign with classic crest, dating to the 1960s, sold for $4,500.

Reliable Premium Regular 13-1/2" lenses in the original Capco globe body, $7,700.

Vespa Service scooter sign with logo, 31" in diameter, $1,500.

Shell (shark-tooth shape) sign, 48" x 48", $1,750.

Shell milk glass globe, $600.

Speedwell Motor Oil porcelain flange sign with "Running Made Easy" logo, $600.

Hard-to-find Studebaker Rockne Authorized Service Genuine Parts sign with logos, $3,500.

A rare autographed Marilyn Monroe calendar featuring the young model stretched out in her "New Wrinkle" pose advertises the Los Angeles Paramount Paint & Lacquer Co. It is signed and inscribed to Mary Karger, sister of Fred Karger, Marilyn's vocal coach at Columbia Studios and one of her early love interests. Measuring 33" x 16", the poster sold at auction for $5,000.

Gold Carnation is the ninth in the series of 12 "Legacy Nudes" that pin-up artist Alberto Vargas (American, 1896-1982) painted for his wife Anna Mae in the 1940s, a low point in their lives after he was fired by *Esquire* and before he began his long association with *Playboy*. Vargas is reported to have considered this series his best work. It sold at auction for $89,625.

CHAPTER 6

NSFW

RACY ART, PULPS, AND NOVELTIES

You might be surprised to learn that many mainstream illustrators and cartoonists got their start in, ahem, "off color illustrations." Carl Barks, who went on to perfect the persona of Uncle Scrooge for Walt Disney comic books, and Theodore Geisel, aka Dr. Seuss, both made their early cash on risqué cartoons and the like for men's magazines. Kinda puts "Hop on Pop" in a whole new light, doesn't it? Anywhoo … the point is that there is a deep and diverse field of smut to collect and the deeper you dig, the more interesting it gets.

Racy art and novelties are as old as horndogs themselves. Art from Pre-Columbian civilizations celebrated the human form as early as 15,000 years ago. The ancient Greeks perfected the practice by adding racy images to every kind of fixed object. Asian cultures were no different. From Japan's erotic prints and ivory netsuke figures to China's jade carvings, the effort to depict the down and nasty was a top artistic subject.

Purveyors wasted no time in adapting the technological advancements of the late 19th centuries to risqué art. The commercialization of the printing press and the advent of photography (especially in 1880s-90s France) made sharing naughty material profitable. A renaissance in NSFW novelties and art exploded in the 20th century: From Tijuana bibles to Gil Elvgren and Alberto Vargas to Bettie Page and Marilyn Monroe, the celebration of the human form and the "bow chicka wow wow" has never been the same.

BAD TASTE OFTEN TASTES GOOD AFTER 50 YEARS.

-Jim Linderman, Vintage Sleaze Blog

Stag magazines and racy pulps were popular for more than 40 years, peaking during the 1960s. Men's pulp magazines were decorated with painted covers full of sexual tension, action, he-men, and sultry damsels in distress. Beyond the cover and a few suggestive interior drawings, guys really picked up pulps "for the articles." In fact, they launched careers for some of the most famous writers of the 20th century including Richard Matheson, Robert Heinlein, Ray Bradbury, Kurt Vonnegut Jr., Philip K. Dick, Robert Bloch, and Harlan Ellison.

Pulps published during World War II switched to digest size to conserve paper, but there were bigger changes afoot as the entire men's publishing landscape changed in the 1950s. Stiff (sorry) competition from glossies spelled the demise of the remaining pulp magazine market and in 1953, the first issue of *Playboy* hit newsstands. From a printing of just over 50,000 copies for this first issue, *Playboy*'s print run reached 5 million within 15 years. Magazines that popped up (I can't help it!) in the 1960s tried to follow suit (*Man*, *Bachelor*, *Modern Man*, *Gent*, *Rouge*, and *Cavalier* among others), with artistic shots of models. The results seem kitschy by today's standards, but they remain a heck of a lot of fun to collect.

It would have been rare in 1976 to find a wall in a teenage boy's bedroom that didn't have Farrah Fawcett in her red swimsuit plastered to it. The iconic, record-breaking poster sold 20 million copies and helped make Farrah an international star.

Another mandatory piece of wall art for Middle-American males was this classic 1978 "pink bikini" poster of supermodel Cheryl Tiegs, which also became an iconic image of 1970s pop culture.

Think you've seen it all? Think again. Years before Carl Barks drew Uncle Scrooge and Donald Duck for Walt Disney Comics, he did risqué gags in magazines such as *Ballyhoo*. He was also known for his mischievous bits of artwork done while at the early Walt Disney Studios. It measures 10" x 13" and sold at auction for $2,300.

WHERE TO LEARN MORE

💋 A strong collecting base has emerged for these items, which are pursued for both tease and social commentary, such as the case of Jim Linderman, who maintains the obscurities-laden Vintage Sleaze Blog, vintagesleaze.blogspot.com.

💋 Few auction houses deal in risqué or racy novelties, but Hakes Americana & Collectibles of York, PA, offers quality collections at least twice a year; Hakes.com.

💋 A warehouse full of vintage novelties and art can be found on a regular basis on eBay.com.

The Marilyn Monroe cover and nude photo spread inside ensured Hugh Hefner's first edition of *Playboy* magazine would get noticed. This is one of the finest copies of the newsstand edition to ever surface and it sold at auction for $55,000.

A collection of 10 color prints, many taken from calendars, sold at auction for $16.

Once collectors complete a set of books, they often turn to original art. This oil on canvas by Hugh Joseph Ward (American, 1909-1945) was painted for the cover of the pulp magazine story "The Evil Flame." It was published in August 1936 as the cover of *Spicy Mystery Stories*. The painting measures 28-1/5" x 19-1/2" and is shown with a copy of the original magazine. From the estate of collector John McLaughlin, the painting sold at auction for $143,400.

This collection of early issues of *Playboy* – every copy from 1954 through 1956 – contains 35 separate issues. Why not 36? Curiously, *Playboy* did not publish an issue in March, 1955; $4,062.

Party After Hours was released in 1955 and remains one of the rarest 10-inch albums produced by Aladdin. The red vinyl record contains risqué material loaded with double entendres in songs performed by the best of the label's roster (Amos Milburn, Wynonie Harris, "Crown Prince" Watterford, and Velma Nelson). One of the all-time classic early rhythm and blues rarities, the album sold at auction for $4,780.

This group of pulp magazines spans the years 1928 to 1941 and includes the comically named *Eyeopener's Annual Red Pepper* from 1937. The set sold at auction for $89.

Candidate Al Smith and the Democrats favored the repeal of the 18th Amendment, which put them at odds with the more sober Republicans. This 1-1/4" button may be only one of two known in the world. It sold at auction for an astounding $8,962. Poor Al didn't win, but Prohibition was finally repealed in 1933.

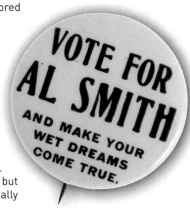

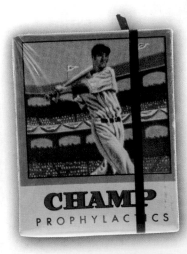

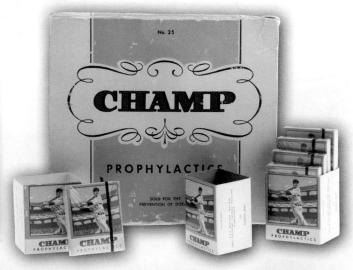

Despite Ted Williams' strong Catholic New England fan base, the makers of Champ brand prophylactics figured it would be a good idea to use The Kid's image to help folks keep from having kids themselves. This assortment of pieces from the marketing campaign made unauthorized use of Williams' image. The set sold at auction for $537.

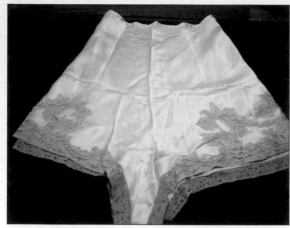

Legend has it that the panties belonging to Adolf Hitler's girlfriend, Eva Braun, were looted from his mountain top chalet called the Eagle's Nest in Obersaltzburg, Germany. First Lieutenant D.C. Watts of the 506th Parachute Infantry Regiment claimed the delicates on May 6, 1945, which is fully documented in Chase Haddock's *Treasure Trove, The Looting of the Third Reich*. The panties were worn by Ms. Braun, presumably laundered, and returned to her bureau where Lt. Watts liberated them. These were found in Ernie Scarano's Mantiques shop in Elmore, Ohio. The price? You'll have to take a road trip to find out.

Mens' minds have been in the gutter since the species, well, crawled out of the gutter. But what happens when a father and son, Franz Xaver Bergman Sr. and Jr., own a bronze foundry about 100 years before *Playboy*? They churn out a line of sculptures such as this one that are the 19th century equivalent to a mullet: business in the front, party in the back. "Wearing a Coat," Vienna, Austria, circa 1900, unmarked, 6-7/8" h, $4,182.

The 1961 "sexploitation" film, *Nude on the Moon*, features a moon colony filled with telepathic nude women. This one sheet movie poster sold at auction for $669.

Back to Nature was one of the earliest nudist documentaries ever made and features footage shot in nudist camps all over the world. Among the places showcased in the 1933 flick are nudist camps in upstate New York, nudist nightclubs in France, and a retreat in Germany that is claimed to be the world's largest nudist camp. The film was banned in New York State on public decency laws. Very few copies of this poster survived from the film's very small distribution. Mounted on linen, the poster sold at auction for $3,346.

72 MANTIQUES *A Manly Guide to Cool Stuff*

CHAPTER
7

MID-CENTURY BACHELOR PAD
COLLECTING MID-CENTURY MODERN

Carlos Cardoza's spent nearly 20 years hunting for mantiques at flea markets, eBay, antiques shops, and garage sales to outfit his Mid-Century Modern home. His attention to detail has landed his house on HGTV and multiple newspaper and magazine spreads. The best part: He uses every single square foot of the home. The collection is not in his way and makes his life better for one reason or another.

"I love using my things," Carlos says. "If I can't use it, then I don't buy it."

Carlos doesn't collect antiques. He collects great 20th century design. His custom-built 1954 home is the largest item in his collection. It is in-

OPPOSITE PAGE TOP: Living with great art is easy when you're an artist. Carlos' own painting hangs above a red Paul McCobb sofa with original brass frame, a Corona chair and ottoman designed by Poul Vother circa 1958-1960, and a Noguchi coffee table. The lamp is an iconic Triennale floor lamp by Arredoluce of Monza, Italy. The circa 1950s masterpiece is made of chromed-plated brass, enameled steel, and aluminum, and can be found at auction for $7,000 to $12,000.
OPPOSITE PAGE BOTTOM: Bookended by a George Nelson for Howard Miller vintage ball clock and a George Nelson cigar lamp hangs another one of Carlos' original paintings. On the table next to the platform sofa is an Ericofon by Ericsson Co. valued at about $100. The lime green chair to the far left is a George Nelson Coconut Lounge Chair, circa 1955, valued at about $2,000.

Carlos chilling in a classic La Chaise lounge as designed by Charles and Ray Eames in 1948 for an international competition sponsored by the Museum of Modern Art. The contest challenged the 20th century's top designers to create the most stylish low-cost furniture design.

WHERE TO LIVE?

To really pull off a great collection of Contemporary and Space Age design, you really need a Mid-Century home. Architecture from the atomic age can be found in most urban cities since many tastemakers found a way to introduce the look during the housing boom of the 1950s and 1960s. This is especially true of areas that saw heavy development following World War II, such as Dallas and Las Vegas. However, a few cities have notable concentrations of classic Mid-Century Modern homes: Los Angeles and Palm Springs, Calif.; Denver, Colo., Miami, Fla.; London.

fused with Modernism, Contemporary, Post Modern, and Space Age finds great and small. Much of it is influenced by his upper middle class upbringing smack dab in the 1950s—a busy design decade eager to shrug off a depressing world war, while diving headfirst into rebellion and affluence. He effortlessly combines all of his finds into a Mid-Century showcase that spans 60 years worth of design. He even kept his iMac G4 from 2002, Apple's hemispherical flower pot-style personal computer.

His collection includes a stunning 1958 Glass Magic Playmaster boat with large fins, which he's been known to tow with his pink, 1960 Cadillac Series 62. In his dining room hangs a 1942 leg splint designed by Charles and Ray Eames.

"This was the first molded plywood

A set of six Cone chairs by Verner Panton is accompanied by a George Nelson flying saucer pendant hanging light. The sculpture in the corner of the room is an authentic molded plywood leg splint as designed by Charles and Ray Eames for soldiers during World War II. You earn major street cred having a leg splint hanging in your dining room.

The kitchen retains most of its original cupboards and 1950s pink appliances, but Carlos installed the stainless steel backsplash. The home's bar—an iconic design addition for the era—is stocked with cocktail glasses and trays found at garage sales and on eBay.

In February 1968, *Look Magazine* featured a spread of Richard Avedon portraits of The Beatles that had been decked out with psychedelic effects. Readers had a chance to buy enlargements and in Carlos' home office, a complete set is on display above a 1960s Japanese Weltron 2003 yellow globe 8-track stereo. It all comes together with a classic Broyhill Premier yellow plastic dresser, based in part on a design by Raymond Loewy.

piece designed by the Eameses during World War II. The splint was the start of that design process and from this came the famous furniture designs," he says.

The splint hangs in a corner next to a table surrounded by a set of Cone chairs from 1959, as produced by designer Verner Panton in 1958. A mantiques collector like Carlos looks for furniture that's cool and collected but practical and unexpected. Remember, the table you can't set a drink on belongs at Grandma's.

Harry Bertoia chairs are grouped with a 1960s-era metal patio umbrella near the home's classic kidney-shaped pool. Instead of boring fountain or waterfall, Carlos built a custom base for an 8-foot concrete advertising figure of Big Boy, mascot of the famous restaurant chain.

A spare bedroom is devoted to toys and other collections. Carlos' custom bicycle creations, one devoted to Roy Rogers and another, a replica of Pee-wee Herman's infamous bike, were built around modern Huffy and Schwinn replicas.

Vintage and repro tin litho robots and cars by companies like Schuco are displayed in a spare bedroom. The turquoise Womb chair and ottoman were designed by Eero Saarinen in 1948.

WHERE TO LEARN MORE

✳ You know where Mid-Century Modern buffs hang out? Pinterest. Search "mid century décor" for images and links to famous (and not so famous) homes and cool objects all across the country; don't miss the Mid Century Home board from Amsterdam: http://pinterest.com/midcenturyhome.

✳ *Atomic Ranch Magazine*: www.atomic-ranch.com, the publication of record on the architecture and attitude of Mid-Century Modern homes and their owners.

$750-$800

This Alvar Aalto laminated birch dining table was designed in Finland. Despite that, it originates from 1930—the very early part of the mid-century movement. The table would look great in a Mid-Mod home. It measures 29" x 48-1/2" and can be found for $750-$800.

$380

Another set from Alvar Aalto, this set of four laminated birch stools, Model No. 63 for Finmar, were actually produced 20 years apart: one came from the 1930s and the other from the 1950s. Standing 30-3/4" h, the set sold for $380.

$9,560

This walnut single-pedestal desk was made in the 1960s by designer and furniture maker George Nakashima, king of Mid-Mod organic furniture. Measuring 28-3/4" x 63-1/4" x 25-1/8", it sold for $9,560 at auction.

$1,500

A fantastic walnut dining table and four upholstered walnut chairs designed by "America's Decorator" Paul McCobb in the 1950s. The table is 29" x 60" x 38" and each chair is 34" x 18" x 17". The set sold for $1,500 at auction.

These bedside tables date to the 1950s and are Italian. They are marked Esse VI on the glass, measure 23-3/4" x 22-1/2" x 14", and sold for $4,180 at auction.

Wood and metal floor lamp, circa 1950, 65" h, sold for $1,800.

Just like the one in Carlos' collection, these Egg chairs and ottoman were designed by Arne Jacobsen (Danish, 1902-1971) and manufactured by Fritz Hansen, Copenhagen, Denmark, circa 1958. They are marked FH, BY FRITZ HANSEN, MADE IN DENMARK, DANISH FURNITURE MAKERS CONTROL, 1163 and stand 42" x 33-3/4" x 18-1/2". The set is valued at more than $5,000. This organically shaped chair was originally designed by Jacobsen for the lobby and reception areas of the SAS Royal Hotel in Copenhagen in 1958.

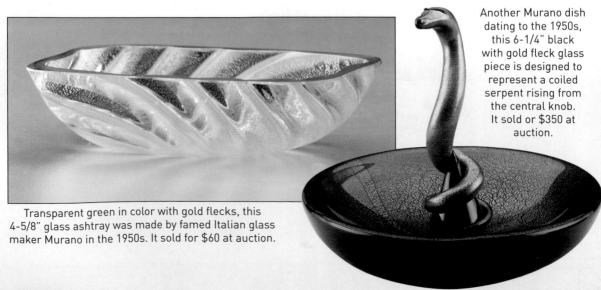

Another Murano dish dating to the 1950s, this 6-1/4" black with gold fleck glass piece is designed to represent a coiled serpent rising from the central knob. It sold or $350 at auction.

Transparent green in color with gold flecks, this 4-5/8" glass ashtray was made by famed Italian glass maker Murano in the 1950s. It sold for $60 at auction.

Pin-Up in Turquoise Bikini, Gil Elvgren (American, 1914-1980), Simoniz advertisement, circa late 1950s/early 1960s, oil on canvas, 20" x 38-1/4". It sold for $71,500 at auction.

Designed by Sweden's Ericsson Telephone Company in the late 1940s, the Ericofon or the Cobra Phone was originally designed for hospital use due to its ease of use, according to mega-collector's Richard Rose's Ericofon website. $75-$100 for rarer colors.

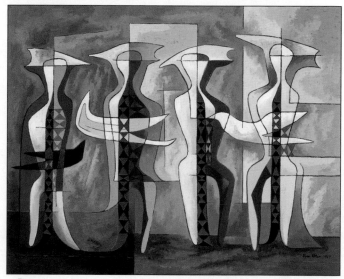

Presence, October 1957, Bror Alexander Utter (American, 1913-1993), oil on canvas, 24" x 30", sold for $9,560 at auction. Bror Utter was a leading member of a group of modernists called the Fort Worth Circle of Artists who dominated the avant-garde art scene in the 1930s and 1940s.

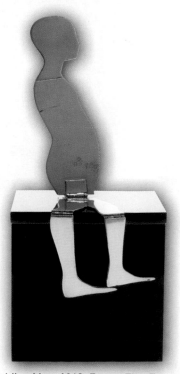

Folding Man, 1969, Ernest Tino Trova (American, 1927-2009), solid brass hinged figure contained in Perspex box; folding man: 12-1/2" x 4-1/2"; box: 5" x 5" x 5". $800-$1,000. Trova, an artist whose signature creation, a gleaming humanoid known as "Falling Man," appeared in a series of sculptures and paintings and became a symbol of an imperfect humanity hurtling into the future.

George Nelson & Associates Eye clock, model 2238, made by the Howard Miller Clock Company in 1957 of brass, enameled brass, walnut, enameled steel, enameled aluminum and awesomeness. It measures 30-1/4" w x 2-1/2" d x 13-1/2" h and often sells in the $1,500 to $3,000 range. You can find modern repros from China ... but what fun is that?

Includes: Yone Swinging Baby Robot; MTU Cap-Tain, the Robot; large Ideal plastic robot; Noguchi paddle walking robot; Linemar Robotrac robot tractor; a pair of battery-operated robots. The Yone is 12" h (with sign in place), litho tin, windup; the Cap-Tain is 5-1/2" h, litho tin windup in box; the Ideal large plastic robot 14" h; Noguchi paddle walking windup robot is 5-1/2" h; Linemar Robotrac is tin, 9-1/2" l x 6-1/2" h; and the two tin litho mechanical robots are 12" h. This set sold at auction for $71, but a set as large as Carlos' could cost you several hundred bucks.

Mr. Atom, a classic plastic robot, was made by Advance Doll & Toy in 1956. He comes with his original box, stands 18" h and can be found online and in toy auctions for $125.

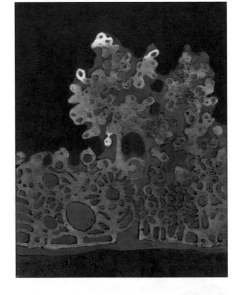

Ombú, Nicholás García Uriburu (Argentinean, b. 1937), oil on masonite, 17-3/4" x 13-3/4", $5,975. Uriburu specializes in stylized nature paintings and "land art."

Modeled as a chrysanthemum flower on a fluted pedestal base, this silver tazza was designed by Samuria Shokai, Yokohama of Japan. It is 6-1/2" in diameter, weighs 10.3 ounces, and is marked SAMURAI SHOKAI., YOKOHAMA., STERLING., (Japanese mark). It sold for $320 at auction.

Cityscape, circa 1950s, Fabiani (French, 20th century), oil on canvas, 23" x 47", sold for $487 at auction.

Cat Lady, unpublished science-fiction digest cover, circa 1950s, Hannes Bok (American, 1914-1964), watercolor and gouache on paper, 9-3/4" x 6-1/4", sold for $11,875 at auction. Bok painted over 100 covers for various science fiction, fantasy, and detective fiction magazines and was the first artist to win the Hugo Award.

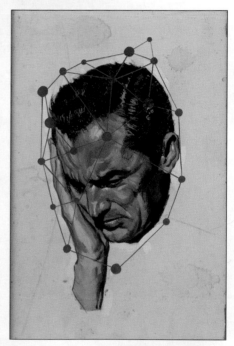

A personal favorite, Untitled (*Thinking Man*) is an original illustration by Bernard D' Andrea (b. 1923). It measures 9" x 6-1/4" and sold for $180 at auction.

Arcs from Four Corners, 1986, color woodcut on Echizen Torinoko paper by Sol Lewitt (American, 1928-2007), 8-1/2" x 28-1/2", sold for $2,750 at auction.

Art Deco: The Masculine Movement

For design purposes, the term Mid-Century Modern applies to objects made between 1933 and 1965. It is an umbrella term that tries to cover a major design trend that took place in the United States and Europe, with important contributions from designers in Scandinavian countries. Tucked inside this term you find subset design movements and styles such as the bright and colorful Scandinavian designs of the 50s and 60s and the smooth and angular Art Deco.

Art Deco homes and furnishings have plenty of mantique appeal. The style first appeared in France in the 1920s, but quickly spread during the Great Depression and fell out of favor after World War II. Great design doesn't lose its appeal and Art Deco objects are collected by themselves or as additions to any manner of collections and interiors.

This circa 1935 lamp with solid black glass base and hemispherical green shade painted with black enamel is probably from Austria. It stands 11-1/2" h and sold for $625 at auction.

These circa 1935 ringed torpedo-form lamps rising from a hemisphere on stepped base measure 23" x 18" and sold for $2,125.

A very cool chromed metal and glass airplane lamp from SARSAPARILLA, DECO DESIGNS by Ray A. Schober is 12" l, and sold for $468.

Designed by John Vassos (American, 1898-1985) and manufactured by RCA, New York, New York, 1936, this floor radio stands 40" h and sold for $5,000.

These circa 1930 marbleized orange bookends with green triangular element, standing 6-1/3" h, sold for $406 at auction.

Made by Art Metal of Newark, N.J., circa 1930, this kick-ass brass cigarette dispenser has a faux tortoiseshell cylindrical body, raising on spring to reveal holders for individual cigarettes, enameled brass bartender to top. It stands 7-7/8" h and sold for $275 at auction.

The American Cabinet Co., of Two Rivers, Wis., produced some pretty amazing furniture in the 1930s. This art deco enameled metal dentist cabinet stands 50-1/8" x 40" x 15" and sold for $625.

This Art Deco Manning-Bowman chrome coffee percolator was made in Booneville, Missouri. It stands 15" h and can be found for about $100.

Seeburg Symphonola jukebox in black lacquer and silvered case, circa 1940, 50-1/4" h x 30-1/2" w x 20-3/4" d, $2,000-$3,000.

A black Aaron brand fedora owned and worn by Frank Sinatra, with his name and "Sands Hotel" embossed on the sweatband. Sold at auction for $3,883.

This Patek Philippe Platinum Diamond Dial Watch was made for Tiffany & Co., circa 1940, and sold for $8,125 at auction.

SHARP-DRESSED MAN
FASHION ACCESSORIES

Collecting vintage fashion is more about picking unusual and distinctive accessories, rather than dressing like a 1960s-era corpse. Yes, you're looking for cool neckties, vintage Chucks, or cool lapel pins or cuff-links. No, you're not seeking brown suits that smell like that one weird corner of Goodwill reserved for drapes no one wants and floral seat cushions haunted with the ghosts of a thousand farts.

It's hard to pull off a full vintage suit what with a revolution taking place in 21st century fashion. Lapels are getting thinner on modern suits and the cut is far too slim. A vintage men's fashion collector looks awesome in a modern suit accented with a cool 1950s painted necktie and vintage cuff-links. A hipster wearing a full-blown suit is still a hipster in a suit.

Fashion is an area a collector can break down walls. I once watched a 24-year-old shopper named "Hiro," from Japan, browse a booth of folk art, industrial grunge, and advertising during a rainy Brimfield Antiques Show in Brimfield, Mass. Other than a nod, he and the dealer didn't seem to have much in common. That is, until, Hiro spotted two vintage Harley-Davidson leather jackets hanging from a cord. He cocked his head to the right like a dog on point and after a quick haggle, he walked with both for $650.

This circa 1960s Swiss-made Elgin watch is about as unique as it gets for a personal timepiece. It has an automatic chronograph with digital hours and minutes and sold for $1,062 at auction.

Hiro with one of the leather jackets he scored at Brimfield.

The vintage leather jacket is probably the most ubiquitous mantique clothing item in collections. Pick a decade and you can find a leather jacket that represents the time period better than any other item of men's fashion. As expected, the hottest and most valuable jackets are those that represent their era the best. Wanna rock it like the Greatest Generation? Pick up some WWII leather flight jackets. Want to show your dad how you can make his leather look great again? Hunt down a black Harley-Davidson ass-kickin' rockabilly jacket. Even stage-worn leather jackets by well-known heavy metal groups can be owned for less than $2,000.

Another hot area of men's fashion is vintage neckties. Dealers can't keep them in stock.

"Our usual consumers are men between the ages of 25 to 45, ranging from traditional collectors to architects, from lawyers to graphic artists—people from all different backgrounds and with varying tastes," said Alyssa Duffy, of The Vutique, a Seattle online retailer of vintage fashion and funky finds. "What we usually see the wearer go for are designs—colors, the width of the tie—depending on that individual's taste."

Some chalk it up to the impact AMC's *Mad Men* has on pop culture, but vintage ties were popular long before Don Draper showed up.

"I believe a vintage tie can work with any suit," said Dennis Tuazon, owner of Sewmanity of Alameda, Calif. His Etsy shop is filled with vintage neckties with prices starting at $20. "It depends on the personality of the wearer. Skinny, striped, or something from the '40s with a hula dancer on it all works if you're willing.

Once a gentleman secures the means, vintage watches make a great investment. The most attractive aspect of modern wristwatches is not based on their ability to tell the time. There, I said it. Let's face it: you can look at your phone if you want to find the time. With that out of the way, the basic decisions you need to make when picking out watches to wear or collect are makers, materials, eras, and price. Got $20,000 to spend on a watch? Buy the very best you can afford. Read reference books such as *The Watch* by Gene Stone. Call a reputable auction house and ask to speak to the watch specialist. You need an expert in your corner and watch specialists have seen it all. They can tell you that it will come down to personal style. Some gentlemen stick to models made by Patek Philippe, say a Calatrava as a day-to-day workhorse and a Aquanaut for relaxing.

Picking Pateks

GOOD

This Patek Philippe & Co. custom wristwatch at left has a 44 mm stainless steel case, curved lugs, a transparent back, and brought $3,750 at auction.

Circa 1949 Patek Philippe (Ref. 1463) very fine, rare and important 18k yellow gold gentlemen's chronograph, features an inclined and stepped bezel, 35 mm, concave lugs, screwed-down case back, inner dust protection cap, round push buttons. This watch was made solely for sale in the United States and likely for an important client. It brought $98,500 at auction.

BETTER

The above Patek Philippe platinum wristwatch (Ref. 5004P) is considered extremely rare and important. Features include split-seconds chronograph, registers, perpetual calendar, moon phases, leap year adjustment and 24-hour indication. It sold for $242,500 at auction.

BEST

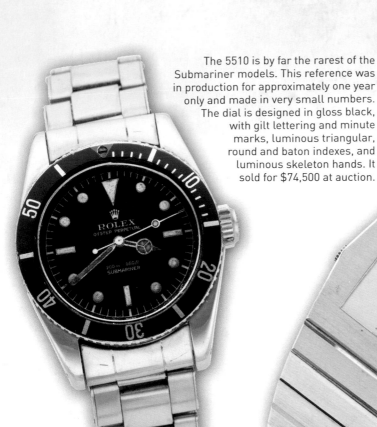

The 5510 is by far the rarest of the Submariner models. This reference was in production for approximately one year only and made in very small numbers. The dial is designed in gloss black, with gilt lettering and minute marks, luminous triangular, round and baton indexes, and luminous skeleton hands. It sold for $74,500 at auction.

This gold Rolex Cellini King Midas Integral bracelet wristwatch, circa 1967, was owned and worn by John Wayne. It sold for $26,200 at auction.

An easily obtained but classically designed Rolex gent's steel oyster perpetual wristwatch can be found at auction for $2,000 to $3,000.

A stunner of a watch truly befitting the Presidential moniker, this circa 1978 diamond white gold Rolex President self-winding wristwatch sold for $23,900 at auction. Total carat weight of the gems on the dial, bracelet and case is 26.35 carats. More ice than a hockey ring!

In close competition with Rolex's Steel Oyster as probably the most collectible mantique watch is the Cartier Tank wristwatch. It was created by Louis Cartier in 1917 who designed its lines and proportions similar to the actual tanks used on WWI battlefields. Mantiques collectors covet this watch and no matter which decade you pick, the Tank is an iconic representation of the era's design. It can be found at auction for $2,000-$3,500, depending on condition. The version pictured here is an 18 karat gold model from the 1980s, which sold for $2,523.

Picture yourself at your next corporate presentation, reaching for a pen as your sleeve hikes up and out pops one of these bad boys. You're not ashamed because life is too short to wear a boring watch. This circa 1948 Gene Autry automated watch (with automated pistol) and this circa 1918 Elgin (Swiss) grid case watch, were sold together at auction for a paltry $450.

This unique gentleman's wristwatch is a manual wind made by HP. It has a stainless steel case and sold for $437 at auction.

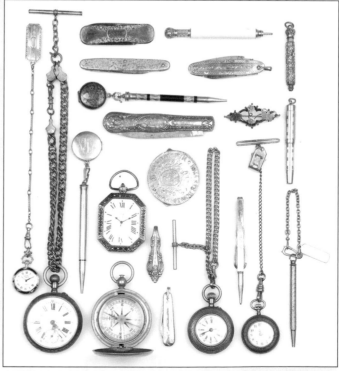

It's not surprising vintage fashion buffs keep small, but important, side collections. Various watches (pocket or wrist), pocket knives, or other odds complete the look and back in the day few true gentlemen would be caught dead without these items. This collection of mantique pocket watches, pens, knives, and a compass sold for $600 at auction.

How to Pick a Vintage Tie

Measure everything

Measurements are highest priority; patterns and colors come second. No matter if you like something bold or something subtle, pay attention to the proportions. Measure the widest part of your tie and the widest part of the lapel of your chosen suit. They should be equal in proportion. Choose a tie that fits your personality and the environment you'll be in. Hint: Modern ties are 58-1/2" long.

Be picky

There is such a thing as a rare necktie, so be picky about the condition of the one you purchase. Most dry cleaning establishments can clean silk, but you can tell when a tie is tired and has had it.

Don't break the bank

Men have been wearing ties for a long time and they're everywhere when you know where to look. Start with your local thrift store or hit up an estate sale.

Look for you

Pick up ties that appeal to you and your personality. Consider sticking to a theme such as silk ties from the '40s era with wide elaborate designs or of traditional regimental stripes. Collect what you like; follow a theme, or select ties you could easily work into your wardrobe. If you would like to collect rare or unusual vintage, do some research on value.

When in doubt, buy the brand

Hermès tops the list. You will never wrong with a vintage Hermès tie. Other popular designers whose work stands the test of time include Dior, Gucci, and Pucci, Yves Saint Laurent, and Brooks Brothers. They're more favorable because of their design emphasis featuring iconic logos and signature graphics.

It doesn't get cooler than this 1940s Space Age-hand-painted rocket tie. At 52-1/2" l x 3-1/2" w the labels reads, "Hand Painted by Andre of California-Hand Tailored," and "Al's Hat Shop, 863 Broadway, Buffalo, NY." It was offered for $150.

From left: 1940s hand-painted bird tie, $75; Cardinal Ballerina dancers tie from the '50s, $55; signed on the print Salvador Dali tie, $185.

Don't mess with the oil rigs. This all silk wide swing necktie dates to the 1940s and is decorated with oil derricks. It measures 4-1/2" across its widest point, and is 51" l. It can be found for about $75.

Burberry silk vintage tie, 4" w, 57 1/4" l. Tags: Burberrys of London, 100% Pure Silk, Hand Sewn in USA, $20.

A crazy wide tie from the disco era, 4-1/4" w x 54" l. Tags: Gino Pompeii, Hand Made in Italy, Terytal, 100% Textured Polyester, $10.

Snag an extra portion of cranberries with this 1950s era crepe silk turkey tie, 4-1/8" w x 51" l. Tags: Exclusively Hand Painted, Hand Painted, Hand Tailored, $15.

Late '40s hand-painted naked island girl tie, $250.

Great looking tie from J. Press, part of the Alpha Beta Collection, 4" w x 54-3/4" l. Tags: Madralyte, 80% Polyester, 20% Cotton, by J. Press, $20.

Brown on brown starburst pattern running vertically down the entire length of the necktie, silk, 2-1/2" w x 55" l. Tags: Andre of California - Hand Tailored, $20.

Minute Mantiques Guide: Cufflinks

Tastemakers have always had a love/hate relationship with cufflinks. That's why collectors have always had a hate/hate relationship with tastemakers. Cufflinks stand the test of time and come in a myriad of styles, themes, metals and gems. You can find them affordably and in some cases even make money on your purchase. While flea sellers are jacking up prices on pot metal necklaces and rings, you often can find platinum on 14 karat yellow gold cufflinks for $10-$50—score!

If you're looking for quantity over quality, then buy what you like. Hundreds of styles were produced from the 1930s to 1960s by costume jewelry makers such as Swank or Dante. If you're looking for quality buys with resale potential, then look for high-end names such as Tiffany, Cartier, and David Webb. The value in cufflinks usually comes from two sources: the quality of the materials and provenance (meaning you can prove the set was previously owned by Elvis or flown to the moon on an Apollo lunar mission).

Did you know you can own a pair of cufflinks once personally owned by Clark Gable for about the same price you can purchase a pair of new links at a chain clothier? If anyone asks you why you have the initials CG on your wrist, just look at them and say: "Maybe they aren't my initials … but they are CLARK GABLE'S!"

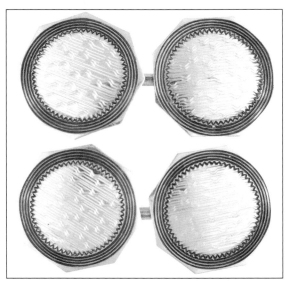

Pair of 1/2" 14k gold cufflinks, gross weight 3.8 grams, personally owned and worn by actor Clark Gable, $336.

Pair of karat gold and enamel "bull's head" cufflinks by David Webb. Each terminal designed as a bull's head, decorated by blue enamel, accented by red enamel eyes, mounted in 18 karat yellow gold, signed, $3,060.

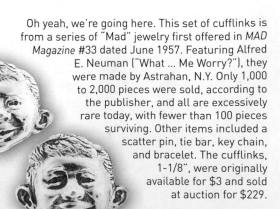

Oh yeah, we're going here. This set of cufflinks is from a series of "Mad" jewelry first offered in *MAD Magazine* #33 dated June 1957. Featuring Alfred E. Neuman ("What … Me Worry?"), they were made by Astrahan, N.Y. Only 1,000 to 2,000 pieces were sold, according to the publisher, and all are excessively rare today, with fewer than 100 pieces surviving. Other items included a scatter pin, tie bar, key chain, and bracelet. The cufflinks, 1-1/8", were originally available for $3 and sold at auction for $229.

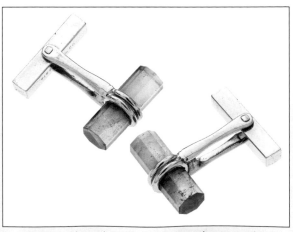

Octagon-shaped aquamarine crystals measuring 18 x 6 mm, set in 14k gold, gross weight 11.40 grams, 1" x 3/4", $717.

This pair of WWII painted leather flight jackets includes an issue A-2 jacket retaining the original leather lieutenant's bars sewn on the shoulder straps. The back has a large 20th Air Force insignia beneath, which is stenciled "Guam." The second is a commercial leather flying jacket with a large 8th Air Force insignia painted on the shoulder of the left sleeve; 527th Bomb Squadron painted leather patch sewn above the left front pocket; and the reverse is painted with the aircraft name "Bits 'n Pieces" and eleven bombs indicating missions, and one (hard to see) flaming aircraft indicating an aerial kill. The pair sold for $956.

WWI-era black leather flying coat with sheepskin collar, three quarter-length, displays some characteristics found in European flying jackets of the period. Dark gray wool lining and sheepskin shawl-type collar. Single breasted with four plastic front buttons. Two upper slash pockets and two lower large flap pockets. Belted. Button cuffs with jersey lining. Looks similar to German examples from the period, $627.

"King of Rockabilly" and Rock and Roll Hall of Famer and all around hell raiser Gene Vincent's own Harley-Davidson leather biker's jacket was once on exhibit at the Metropolitan Museum of Art in New York City, The Beatles Story Museum in Liverpool, England, and the Rock and Roll Hall of Fame and Museum in Cleveland, once sold for $7,767.

The 14k yellow gold money clip has a woven design and a gross weight 28 grams. It measures 2-1/4" x 1" and sold for $597.

A Buffalo nickel, aka a hobo nickel, as carved by artist Owen Covert, is set on this sterling silver money clip. It was once in the Troy Wiseman Collection and sold for $149.

John Wayne's 14k gold money clip from the 1950s, in the form of a horseshoe with a horse head in the center, was considered a sign of good luck. Measuring 1-1/2" x 1-1/2", the clip sold for $10,157.

This set of four M. L. Leddys and Resistol cowboy hats (all size 7 3/8) was snapped up for $300 at auction.

A 1940s Borsalino fur felt fedora, $75, alongside a vintage store display for Dunlap hats, c. 1955, $75 each.

Italian straw fedora by Florentine, circa 1950, $89.

Early '60s Bonds velour felt hat with braided band, $78.

The tiled bathroom displays Carlos Cardoza's hat collection, which includes a Davy Crockett coonskin cap and assorted fedoras from the 1950s-60s.

A collection of Carlos Cardoza's Converse Chuck Taylor sneakers have become a mini art installation. Classic pairs from the 1960s can be found from $100 to as much as $1,000 online.

A 1950s Royal Stetson Ivy League fedora, $85.

CHAPTER 9

TECHNETRONIC
COMPUTERS AND OTHER GADGETS

As a collector of vintage typewriters, I am well familiar with the stares and wrinkled noses as people ask: "That's what you collect?" If I'm not in mixed company, my first response is usually "Take off, Hoser!" But a more appropriate response is to say there are as many types of collectors as there are technical antiques to collect.

I'm proud of my typewriters, damn it. Each 40-pound beast is a technological marvel. It's also got a growing fan base among mainstream tech collectors. Tom Hanks is perhaps the best-known vintage typewriter collector and even he's not afraid to share his passion in the pages of *The New York Times*. Neither was I when I spoke of the wonders of typing on a portable for an article in *The Wall Street Journal*. The times are becoming more acceptable for vintage technology collectors, mainly because it's hip to love machines. I give credit for all of this to changing demographics and Apple, Inc.

What does the maker of the first commercially successful (notice I didn't say first) touch pad computing hardware have to do with vintage technology collectors? Lots, if you stop to think that Apple put cutting-edge technology into homes just as the typewriter companies like Royal or Remington or Smith did in the early 20th century. My theory is that the rapid move away from keyboards with a technology so easy to use and, frankly, a little science fiction-y only make people more nostalgic for the technology like typewriters. They are collected, traded, and even snipped apart so their key fronts can be used in jewelry. Truth be told, that's how my wife and I came

OPPOSITE PAGE: A 1983 Apple Lisa-1, the first commercial computer with GUI (graphical user interface), $54,350.

up with the closing costs on our first house: hunting down unsalvageable typewriters and selling parts to jewelry makers. That won't make me popular with purists, but let's be honest: Factories produced millions of typewriters after WWII and that's one of the reasons why new collectors can get into the hobby for as little as $5 for common models from the 1950s and 1960s. Collecting obscure technology, on the other hand, takes serious dollars. Early typewriter inventions, such as the Edison typewriter made by the A.B. Dick, Co. in 1892, can run as much as $13,000. The most valuable vintage typewriter sold at auction is an 1867 Malling Hansen typewriter, which changed hands for $123,125. It was sold by my longtime friend Uwe Breker, founder and owner of Auction Team Breker of Cologne, Germany.

Breker says technical mantiques with the broadest appeal tend to be those that constantly attract new generations of collectors: classic cameras, for example, and photographic memorabilia. Early motion-picture equipment, movie posters, and props are especially popular. Other areas appeal to collectors who identify with items they remember from their childhood, or from their parents' or grandparents' homes.

"Collecting mechanical music instruments such as barrel organs, musical boxes, and

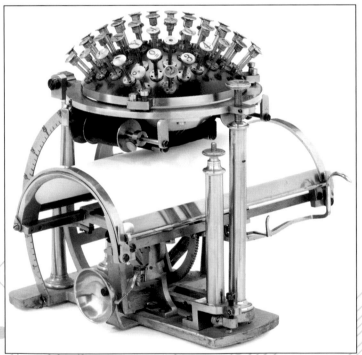

The most valuable vintage typewriter, the 1867 Malling Hansen, sold at Auction Team Breker for $123,125.

The Hermes Media 2 is a Swiss military typewriter produced in 1940. It is a four-row (or four-bank) portable and retains its original wooden military case from the "Pontoon Team of the Truck Convoy 2." It sold for $423 at auction.

A perfect buy for a new collector: the typewriter on the left is a circa 1932 Corona Four in desirable red with a Dutch keyboard, while the machine on the right is a robust British typewriter with universal keyboard called an Imperial Mod. D., dating to 1919. Both sold as a lot for $488.

Odell Type Writer, 1889 Decorative American index typewriter, with typebar and cast nickel-plated base, $734.

Apple II personal computer, $7,033.

gramophones, for example, became popular in the 1950s because that generation had a particular link to pre-war forms of home entertainment," he says. "There is always an element of nostalgia involved."

The ascent of early PC technology is one of the biggest driving changes in the hobby and can be credited with attracting new collectors. An "Apple 1" computer from 1976 reached a new world record price of $671,400 in 2013 after a collector in the Far East bought it for his own tech collection. Although these figures seem staggering, the Apple 1 phenomenon has had quite a steady build up. Early model Apple computers have been changing hands privately for many years, but have only recently started to appear at public auctions. One of the main factors behind the record prices has been condition. Both machines sold by Breker were fully operational computers. According to the *Apple Registry*, there are only 46 Apple 1 units in existence, and of these, just six still work. Combine scarcity, exposure, and historical importance and you've got a recipe for a six-figure computer.

The Apple I was not outstandingly advanced for its time, but it has an historical importance as one of the first affordable home computers. It is also remembered as the first product of the world's most successful company, and the life story of Steve Jobs and Steve Wozniak as two young college drop-outs turned personal computing millionaires.

Interest in office machines, early television, and even the first digital SLR cameras is on the rise, too.

"There was relatively little in print about office antiques such as calculators and typewriters when we started our specialist sales in the mid-1980s," Breker says. "Personal computers were only just becoming affordable. Now all three areas have been accepted into mainstream collecting. The internet has also made it easier for collectors to research, publish, and share their information."

What's hot on the horizon? Smaller format motion-picture cameras (8mm and 16mm), which, until recently, were largely overlooked in favor of earlier 35mm equipment, Breker says. Also look out for the deluxe singing bird musical boxes produced in Switzerland and Germany, especially those decorated with precious metals, gemstones, and enamel. Prices have climbed dramatically over the past 10 years and, judging by recent sales results, they are still rising.

Many collectors are also fascinated by the aesthetic element of technical antiques: the artistry of an automaton from the "La Belle Époque," or the fine engineering of an 18th century English microscope, Breker says. "We have customers from almost every trade: photographers who collect classic cameras, engineers fascinated by Victorian steam models, and doctors with an interest in antique surgical instruments, which today seem curious or even grotesque in comparison to modern technology."

Values can vary widely from one technological mantique to the next. Generally speaking, the three most important factors are quality, rarity, and historical significance. Certain brands command a fierce customer loyalty, whether for their newest or most vintage products. Think Apple computers and the iconic Leica camera.

Another example is the English film manufacturer Ilford, which produced a number of cameras during the post-war years. Its 1952 "Witness" camera was a beautifully engineered, stylish, and commercially unsuccessful (only 350 were produced) competitor of Leica, whereas its "Advocate" camera was simpler and produced for a longer period. Today a Witness could set you back around $17,000, whereas Advocates still regularly change hands for less than $50, Breker says. That's why, as with all mantiques, it pays to do your homework.

SPOTLIGHT

The Original Apple Computer

The Apple 1 was designed and handmade by Steve Wozniak in Silicon Valley and was marketed in April 1976 by Wozniak and Steve Jobs through electronics retail chain, the Byte Shop, which bought the first 50 units.

The Apple 1 was delivered as a motherboard only and is seen here with the very rare original "NTI" logo on the printed circuit board, mean-

This Apple 1 computer from 1976, still in working order, sold for $671,400.

ing it is from the second batch of Apple 1s produced by the duo. The Apple 1 was the first personal computer in the world with monitor and keyboard access. Only 200 were made and just 46 are known to exist. The peripheral equipment, such as power pack, keyboard, monitor, and cassette recorder, all had to be purchased separately. In fact, Wozniak and Jobs never even offered a housing; every user had to make his own.

Instead of an operating system, the Apple 1 employed a monitor program that provided an interface between keyboard entry, the CPU, memory, and monitor exit. Any more sophisticated software system, such as Basic, had to be loaded on cassettes. Therefore, a cassette-interface-card, offered optionally by Apple, was required. This set contains the original card and the original early "6502 micro processor."

Scelbi-8H Mini-Computer Kit, 1973, is arguably the first true personal computer, yet virtually unknown as only three examples survive. This version retains its extensive original documentation from its creator Nat Wadsworth. It sold at auction for $20,780.

MITS Altair 8800, 1975, is known as the first personal computer in the world to be offered in large quantities and is widely considered to be the "first" PC. It was built in 1974 by Ed Roberts and became famous after being featured on the cover of *Popular Electronics* in January 1975. This specimen sold at auction for $11,190.

"Enigma" ciphering machines are hot with collectors. Patented by Dr. Arthur Scherbius and built by Chiffriermaschinen A.G. of Berlin, the iconic three-rotor machine is one of the most complex code-drafting devices ever invented for the German military. Straight from WWII, this 1944 example sold for $35,170.

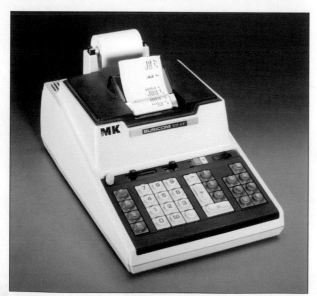

A pioneer electronic calculator containing the first commercial application of an "Intel 4004" processor, the Busicom 141-PF of 1971 sold for $19,200 at auction.

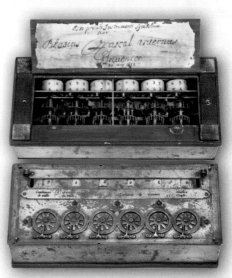

Blaise Pascal, a French physicist, developed a gear-based mechanical machine that accomplished simple computations. Dubbed Pascal's Calculator, this 1920s-era working replica of the 1652 original sold for $41,562 at auction.

A Conto 1912 Swiss toothed-disc adding machine by J. Aumund, Zürich, with eight-digit display, brass case and reset lever with thumb-release. It sold at auction for $1,222.

Models are extremely popular with collectors and the older the better. This working late 19th century brass and wood model of a Victorian-age Beam winding engine stands 31" x 11" x 23" and sold for $6,250 at auction.

Yes, dudes collect pencil sharpeners. This sharpener was made by the Chelsea Mfg. Co. of Chelsea, MI. It employs a sand-disk type field and an automatic pencil rotator. One of these versions once set an auction record when it sold for an astounding $17,200. The one pictured here, however, brought $1,430 at auction last year.

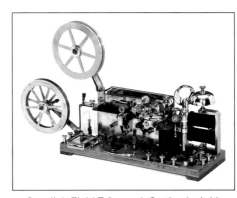

Swedish Field Telegraph Station by L.M. Ericsson, the famous telephone designer and manufacturer, circa 1900, this portable telegraph is a lacquered brass machine with working clockwork drive and a galvanometer, lightning protection, key, and bell. It stands as an exceptionally rare exhibition piece and collector's item in top museum quality. Measuring 15-3/4" x 6-3/4" x 8-1/4", it sold for $2,608 at auction.

This 1895 L.M. Ericsson desk telephone is also known as the "Coffee Grinder" for its distinctive circular shape and lithography. It sold for $19,200.

Demonstration model of Alexander Graham Bell's first telephone, 1976, half-scale reproduction of this historic telephone, 7" x 4" x 6-1/4", $161.

Physical demonstration model of a Watt-type beam engine designed by Eugène Bourdon sold at auction for $7,250.

Age and sophistication are two qualities collectors seek in tech mantiques. This brass equatorial sundial was created by Andreas Vogler in Augsburg, a city in the south-west of Bavaria, Germany, around 1760. The octagonal engraved base with inset compass has an 80-degree side-stand. It's just more than 2" wide and sold for $1,141.

This open-topped racer could be collected both for its French design or its innovative clockwork mechanism. Designed by Eugène Pinard, the distinctive tin car sold for $6,720 at auction.

Coin-op machines are collected for their design and ingenuity. This contraption, labeled "X-Ray Machine For Amusement Only," delivered illustrated gag cards of male and female skeletons, each accompanied by a grim fortune. It sold at auction for $24,000.

Mir Space Station Command Control console and monitor used by both Russian astronauts and cosmonauts in training and preparation for trips to the orbiting space station. There are two components mounted to a 12" x 26" x 10" heavy black metal rack and the top piece is a video monitor of 9-1/2" x 10-1/2" overall dimensions. Beneath is mounted a pushbutton panel of 10" x 7-1/2", with numerous pushbutton keys. It sold for $5,526 at auction.

From Louis XV-style furniture, patinated busts, paintings, a stuffed Bambi and other taxidermied animals shown in the top photo, Rob Bradford's gentleman collection started when he began selling at antiques shows across the country and changes all the time. The table above is home to various odds and ends made up of apothecary jars, a mantle clock, and even an ashtray made from a deer hoof.

CHAPTER 10

WHORE HOUSE MEETS GRANDMA'S HOUSE

COLLECTING VICTORIAN GOTHIC

O K, so we're not in the land of racy magazines or Hot Wheels, but Rob Bradford's collection is mantiques territory all the same. His collection is most accurately described as that of a Gentleman Collector and it is part of a bigger movement worldwide.

Hand-selected auctions of gentlemanly furnishings, luxury accessories, and unique objects have taken hold during the last two years and are now biannual events at the largest fine art auction houses in the United States, England, and across Europe. Several important collections recently made public, including the estates of Malcolm S. Forbes and Vincent Astor, remind us that nostalgia exists for a time when American royalty was created through inheritance or hard work. Who doesn't want a lifestyle suited to travel

Now a costume designer and antiques dealer, Rob Bradford worked in wardrobe for Warner Bros. and also with actress Debbie Reynolds on her Las Vegas show.

Rob Bradford's small apartment is home to a collector's trove of 19th century taxidermy, Victorian Gothic furniture and paintings.

Rob displays more than 30 portraits in his 1,000-square-foot apartment. They aren't the only eyes that follow you around the room. His collection has more than 20 busts in it as well.

and with enough time to pursue scholarly activities without fear of the economic unknown? Isn't that at the heart of most mantiques collections?

Bradford calls his collection New Orleans Style "Whore House meets Grandma's House." "Truthfully, I don't think I paid more than $300 for any one item in the entire place. It's just going out and finding the stuff, which is really getting harder and harder." His favorite haunts are estate sales and flea markets.

The majority of the collection spans the 1820s to 1900, but a lot of contemporary and vintage items are tossed in if they fit. The Victorian fascination with taxidermy is present, with more than 10 pieces spread across multiple rooms. A group of Napoleonic memorabilia grows by happenstance. "All my stuff is blown out and that's how I find it cheap," Bradford says. The opportunity to create a collection fitting of a Victorian gentleman—or a caricature thereof.

"When people think of Victorian, they think of floral patterns, but there's a side that's dark and detached," he says. "I like the detached."

A collection of Napoleonic memorabilia grows by chance, never by effort. "If I see it, I buy it. I'm not looking for anything in particular," Rob says.

This is about as close as these birds would come to this mountain lion mount.

Salvaged from a store display, this pair of gilded plaster hands holds a Victorian beaver top hat amid a sea of 19th century paintings.

The copper bugle was made in 1915 by Whaley, Royce & Co. of Toronto. The daguerreotypes are instant relatives.

$150

$896

A patinated bronze bust of a woman wearing a crown, 14-1/2″, sold at auction for $896.

Renaissance Man by Frederick Millard (British, 1857-1937), oil on canvas laid on board, 8″ x 5-3/4″, $150.

$1,375

This set of leather-bound books, all dating to the early or late 19th century, could be collected for their subject or their binding, which happens to be about Napoleon. The set sold for $1,375.

$4,687

$6,250

In days of old, urns as objects d'art were a must in any quality gentleman's collection. This wooden urn is carved with a floral finial atop a removable lid. It stands 19″ h and sold at auction for $4,687.

French patinated bronze bust of Napoleon, dated 1885, marks: R Columbo, 1885, Paris, TIFFANY & CO. FRANCE, 18″ h, $6,250.

Mantle clocks are popular collectibles, but this particular Victorian-style one was used during the filming of the Gothic soap opera *Dark Shadows*. A hinged glass window opens to allow the hands to be set; it sold at auction for $1,314.

This pair of French kingwood and mahogany bedside cabinets, made circa 1900, sold at auction for $358.

Measuring a full 75" h x 40" w, this Louis XV-style gilt wood mirror was made in France, circa 1900. It sold at auction for $5,312.

Louis XV-style satinwood veneered vitrine cabinet with gilt bronze mounts, made in France, circa 1890. As often found on Louis VX furniture, the ribboned medallions depict Venus and Cupid at the base of either door. It is 70-1/2" x 48-1/2" x 15" and sold at auction for $10,157.

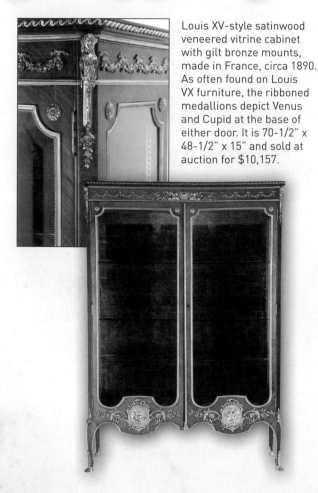

Although it pre-dates the Victorian era by about 200 years, this Italian Renaissance-style walnut, glass, and iron bookcase, dating to the 17th century, would look at home in a Gothic collection. It stands 102" h and sold at auction for $16,250.

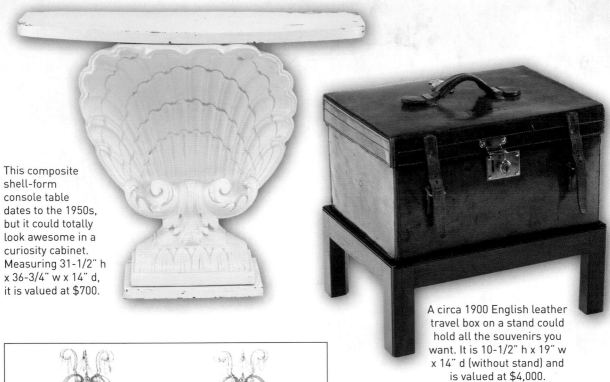

This composite shell-form console table dates to the 1950s, but it could totally look awesome in a curiosity cabinet. Measuring 31-1/2" h x 36-3/4" w x 14" d, it is valued at $700.

A circa 1900 English leather travel box on a stand could hold all the souvenirs you want. It is 10-1/2" h x 19" w x 14" d (without stand) and is valued at $4,000.

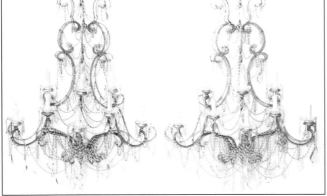

This pair of Continental silvered metal and crystal eight-light sconces, circa 1920, is possibly from France. Measuring 46" x 36" x 19", the pair sold at auction for $1,195.

This American ebonized aesthetic-style slipper chair was likely made in New York, circa 1880. It measures 30-1/4" h x 19" w x 19" d and sold at auction for $1,434.

Probably from France from the early 20th century, this brass and glass tantalus stands 8" h x 10-1/2" w, and sold at auction for $836.

A Victorian top hat was made of beaver by Aborn in Boston during the 1880s. It measures approximately 6" h x 8-1/2" w, and sold at auction for just $50.

A Wedgwood, Burslem (Stoke-on-Trent), Staffordshire, England, figure of a sphinx, made circa 1790-1859, is marked WEDGWOOD and measures 4-1/8" x 6-3/8" x 2-3/8". It sold at auction for $3,107.

This trunk by Louis Vuitton Malletier, Louis Vuitton for short, was made in Paris, circa 1930. It is marked LOUIS VUITTON 870572, measures 34" x 21-1/2" x 9", and sold at auction for $4,375.

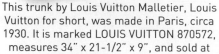

A Victorian walnut and brass fitted box from an unknown maker in England, circa 1880. It is 2-3/8" x 9-1/4" x 6-3/4" and sold at auction for $388.

A shoulder mount of a Pyrenean Chamois (Rupricapra pyrenaica pyrenaica), a species found in the Pyrenees Mountains of southern France and northeastern Spain sold at auction for $209. This species of chamois is quite a challenge to hunt.

This black bearskin rug measures 59" from nose to tail and 61" from paw to paw across. It sold at auction for $956.

Deer Hunt, Sporting Magazine cover illustration, watercolor on board, 16" x 16", $3,883.

CHAPTER 11

THE GREAT OUTDOORS

HUNTING AND FISHING ITEMS

Dan Graf's collection started well before the day he was born.

Graf entered into a family of hunters, fishermen, and truck drivers in the Joppa section of Newburyport, located in northeastern Massachusetts. His grandfather was a Newburyport clam digger and his father and uncle launched one of the largest trucking firms in the region during the 1930s. By the time Dan came along, the Graf family was longtime customers of famous decoy maker Charles Safford (1877-1957) and Dan himself spent his early years learning how to carve decoys from a client of the famous decoy artist George H. Boyd (1873-1941). Dan eventually completed more than 1,000 of his own folk carvings of shorebirds and miniatures, many of which are on display.

But his collection couldn't be limited to only decoys.

Collectibles and artifacts reflecting his deep family roots, a strong respect for the outdoors and Joppa area artists grew to such proportions Dan moved it all to a custom addition built on the back of his garage. Now called "The Museum," the space displays everything from a fine selection of vintage outboard motors to toy trucks, fishing reels to vintage water skis. One corner features a working clam bar. A rare sneak float, an early duck hunting

boat, is on display near the decoy collection.

"One can enjoy collecting almost anything," Dan says. "I believe a true collector collects things they enjoy and have a feel for, not how much it's worth or will be worth. Those people are investors."

At the center of his shrine to the Massachusetts shore is his 40-year collection of George Boyd decoys. His favorite is a hollow-carved, swan-neck goose, but Dan also owns many Boyd miniatures in addition to the actual tools Boyd used to carve his signature decoys.

Boyd, a shoemaker in Seabrook, N.H., carved hunting decoys of ducks, geese, and shorebirds and miniatures in at least 69 species. He sold his miniature carvings for as little as 2 cents to 75 cents when he first carved them in the early 1900s. His talent caught the eye of retailers Abercrombie & Fitch and Macy's, which offered his works in New York. His works now trade at auction for prices ranging from $5,500 to as a much as $20,000. At a 2000 auction held in conjunction with Sotheby's, noted decoy auctioneers Guyette, Schmidt & Deeter set a house record when a rare paddle-tail model of a Merganser drake sold for $77,500. A Boyd paddle-tail model of a red-breasted merganser hen fetched $65,000 during the same auction. The auction record for a Boyd decoy—a canvas covered Canada goose—

is $112,100 at Decoys Unlimited of West Barnstable, Mass., in July 2010.

Dan's appetite for Boyd rarities is well known through the auction circuit. In one instance, he and a friend both so badly wanted to own a Boyd miniature carving that they split the final auction price. For years, every six months, each would send the carving back to the other to enjoy. Talk about dedication and friendship.

Dan's shares his knowledge through exhibitions of Boyd's work or serving as a consultant to books. Perhaps it's one reason why he calls his collection a "museum."

"I'm a collector," he says, "and I hope I always will remain just a collector who enjoys every part of being one."

Hobby is Healthy

Outdoors collectors easily spend millions of dollars a year on rare and pristine examples of classic and modern hunting and fishing collectibles at public auction alone. This doesn't count the stuff found in basements or garages or flea markets and online. There are no rules when it comes to what finds its way into a collection. Well, maybe one rule: It probably shouldn't smell … too badly.

The log cabin home boom of the 1990s and 2000s saw an explosion in cabin décor and a socially acceptable trend in major home design that actually respected a guy's snowshoes on a wall.

Items made or branded by the Winchester Repeating Arms Company are by far the most avidly pursued memorabilia in the hobby. Even magazine pages featuring the company's advertisements are snapped up on eBay. The company made thousands of different items, ranging from flashlights to wagons to clothing, but was especially known for its single-barreled rifles capable of containing multiple rounds of ammunition. Besides the weapons themselves, calendars and die cut signs are among the most sought after of Winchester items. Generally the more elements depicted in a calendar or advertising piece (weapons, animals, manly hunters, and the notoriety of the artist) has a direct relation to the value. But it's the guns collectors are really after. The most popular Winchester gun ever produced was the Model 1873 rifle, "The Gun That Won the West," with more than 720,000 produced. In 2012, Rock Island Auction Co. of Rock Island, Ill., sold an original Half Octagon Half Round Winchester "1 of 1000," estimated to sell between $275,000 to $450,000, for $402,500.

Outside of hunting rifles, a new trend is emerging among collectors: boat motors. These guys are big now and are only expected to gain in popularity. The industrial design of these motors neatly packages streamline aesthetics with mechanical engineering and the color selection and chrome accents add a dash of '50s kitsch.

Lures and Tackle

The allure of classic tackle struck Jerry Zebrowski in 1987. A former CEO, Zebrowski entered retirement with a hunger for reels. His passion quickly grew from pedestrian discoveries to the historical study of fly fishing to pursuing the finest examples ever made. His 316-piece collection, offered at auction in 2008, still stands as one of the finest ever sold as led by a rare George S. Gates raised pillar reel which sold for $14,000. One

A vintage model sail boat, also called a pond sailer or pond yacht, is on display in the collection. The popcorn maker is contemporary as are many of the vehicle models. The sign behind the pond-sailer and the shelves of vintage and contemporary vehicle models pay homage to the family trucking business that was started in the 1930s by Dan's father and uncle. Courtesy Lindsey Bateman; *Hunting & Fishing Collectibles Magazine.*

Decoys and sporting memorabilia fill shelves and cover every corner of an addition Dan added to the back of his garage. Courtesy Lindsey Bateman; *Hunting & Fishing Collectibles Magazine.*

Vintage full-size outboard motors in Dan Graf's museum devoted to the outdoors and the Joppa section of Newburyport, Mass. Courtesy Lindsey Bateman; *Hunting & Fishing Collectibles Magazine.*

feature that sets his collection apart was the amount of thorough research into the variations of markings, styles, and sizes for each reel maker. As his collection matured, Zebrowski only added reels that differed in some small but meaningful way, resulting in a collection comprised mainly of only known examples and one of a kind reels.

Key to Zebrowski's collection was the absolutely pristine collection in which he kept his reels. This rule applies across the board when it comes to fishing lures and tackle: Condition is king. Collectors enjoy looking at mint examples of their favorite lures that may have gotten chewed up, tossed in with a bunch of hooks or snagged on a branch. They may still own those battered lures, reels and rods, but it doesn't mean they want to pay top dollar to display them in their collection.

Made by the Enterprise Manufacturing Co of Akron, Ohio, The Trory Minnow is considered to be one of, if not the, first manufactured wooden underwater minnow, revolutionizing the lure-making industry. Rigged with huge white glass eyes, wire through side treble hooks, and unique square nickel-plated spinners, the lure's paint finish (natural sides, aluminum belly, gold perch stripes, and a dark brown back, tail, and gill mark) is only found on the early Trory Minnows, $21,750.

WHERE TO LEARN MORE

Hunting and Fishing Collectibles Magazine, hfcollectibles.com: Focuses exclusively on collectible artifacts from America's historic hunting and fishing traditions. The bimonthly magazine is fantastic and the links page off the website is everything you need to start collecting or learn more about what you've already got.

Old Fishing Lures & Tackle: Identification and Value Guide, 8th Edition, by Carl F. Luckey Russell E. Lewis.

Finely Carved & Nicely Painted: The Life, Art and Decoys of George H. Boyd, Seabrook, New Hampshire 1873-1941 by Jim Cullen, photography by Andrew Davis; www. georgeboydbook.com.

Classic Hunting Collectibles: Identification & Price Guide by Hal Boggess.

This Truck-Oreno lure in vivid frog spot finish is one of the finest South Bend Lures known to exist. Both the lure and box are in excellent condition, which is why it fetched $10,000 at auction.

Made by Heddon, this Natural Scale Black Suckers lure #1300 still retains its extraordinary natural scale finish. It's 5-3/4" l and has large glass eyes, heavy duty L-rig hardware, and a marked front spinner, $17,750.

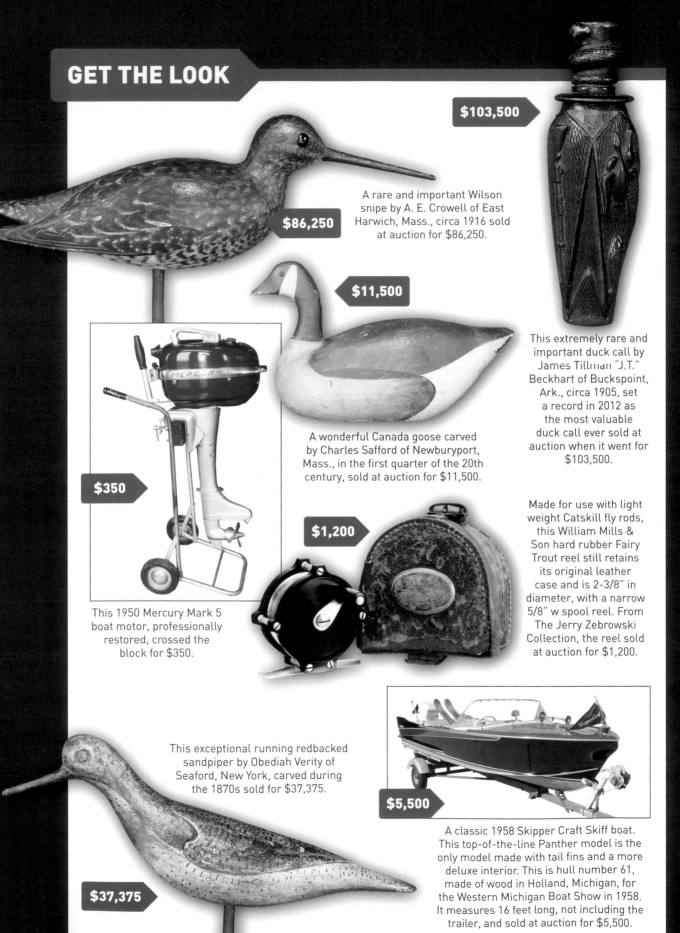

$103,500

$86,250

A rare and important Wilson snipe by A. E. Crowell of East Harwich, Mass., circa 1916 sold at auction for $86,250.

$11,500

This extremely rare and important duck call by James Tillman "J.T." Beckhart of Buckspoint, Ark., circa 1905, set a record in 2012 as the most valuable duck call ever sold at auction when it went for $103,500.

A wonderful Canada goose carved by Charles Safford of Newburyport, Mass., in the first quarter of the 20th century, sold at auction for $11,500.

$350

$1,200

Made for use with light weight Catskill fly rods, this William Mills & Son hard rubber Fairy Trout reel still retains its original leather case and is 2-3/8" in diameter, with a narrow 5/8" w spool reel. From The Jerry Zebrowski Collection, the reel sold at auction for $1,200.

This 1950 Mercury Mark 5 boat motor, professionally restored, crossed the block for $350.

This exceptional running redbacked sandpiper by Obediah Verity of Seaford, New York, carved during the 1870s sold for $37,375.

$5,500

A classic 1958 Skipper Craft Skiff boat. This top-of-the-line Panther model is the only model made with tail fins and a more deluxe interior. This is hull number 61, made of wood in Holland, Michigan, for the Western Michigan Boat Show in 1958. It measures 16 feet long, not including the trailer, and sold at auction for $5,500.

$37,375

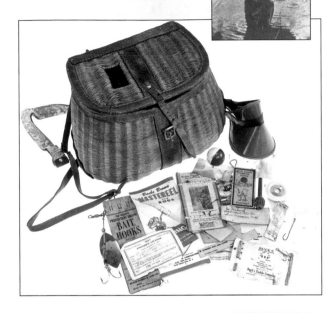

Bing Crosby was an avid angler who often fished while at his Nevada ranch. His wicker-and-leather fishing basket from the 1940s and his angler's license for 1947 sold with some of his fishing line, hooks, lures, floats, and other gear for $956 at auction.

Let's Go Fishing! Saturday Evening Post cover, August 25, 1962, gouache and tempera on board, 17" x 19-1/2", $19,120.

The finest known example of a Heddon lure advertising die-cut display to ever come to auction is this tri-fold, leaping bass with red head shiner scale Zig Wag lure in its mouth. Measuring a remarkable 26" w x 52" h, it opens to reveal a shelf in the middle that the store owner would place Heddon lures in boxes to promote sales. The display is marked copyright 1930, James Heddon's Sons, and Printed by James T. Igoe Co. of Chicago, IL, is printed in the lower right hand corner, $3,000.

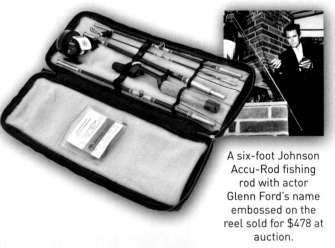

A six-foot Johnson Accu-Rod fishing rod with actor Glenn Ford's name embossed on the reel sold for $478 at auction.

How cool is this? Clark Gable's original 1946 sport fishing license as issued by the State of California, signed twice by the actor and accompanied by the original plastic pin-on holder. It measures 2-1/4" x 3-3/4", $717.

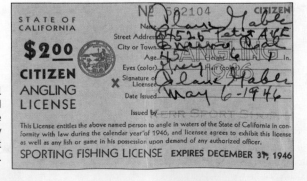

This hunting illustration was sold as a pair with the fishing illustration on the front cover of this book. They are by Bill Gregg (American, 20th Century), mixed media on board, 13" x 20", from the Estate of Charles Martignette, $968.

You can find these Stearns Anglers sports life vest, like the smiling bloke on the cover of this book is wearing, for less than $20 at auction.

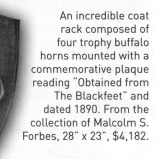

An incredible coat rack composed of four trophy buffalo horns mounted with a commemorative plaque reading "Obtained from The Blackfeet" and dated 1890. From the collection of Malcolm S. Forbes, 28" x 23", $4,182.

Don't call the game warden just yet. This is not a mount of a rare (and generally protected) albino deer. This is a rare subspecies of the Maral deer (Cervus elaphus maral) taken in Bohemia sometime during the late 1800s and early 1900s. Since 1780, these animals have been bred in a rare Bohemian deer park of Schloss Zehusice, home to many species of rare and exotic animals. This perfectly groomed trophy measures 31" h x 38" w, with antlers 24" w, and sold at auction for $1,800.

This French reindeer horn chandelier dates to the early 20th century and features four large stag horn uprights, supported by a ring of five small antlers, having six carved antler candle holders. It measures 35-1/2" x 34" x 34" and is not electrified, but sold at auction for $650.

Decorative and commemorative guns are hotly collected and this exceptional cased pair of Grifnee engraved Holland & Holland Delux game guns are the top of the market. The two 12-guage 2-3/4" Chambers, 28" Chopper lump bbls are engraved "Model Deluxe" on concave game ribs and "Holland & Holland 33, Bruton Street, London." The exceptionally well done scroll work is a backdrop for finely detailed nude portraits of Goddess Diana in various poses with bow drawn. This work was done by noted engraver of the finest guns, the late Philippe Grifnee, whose signature is on each trigger plate. The pair sold for $89,125 at auction.

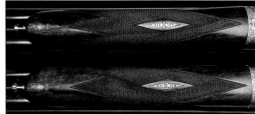

Country stores of the mid-1800s to early 1900s were pretty much a civic center in frontier America. Businesses had limited chances to reach a diverse and largely illiterate customer base, which makes these ammunition cartridge display board so desirable. This one was made to promote the wares of the United States Cartridge Company. It features 99 examples of cartridges, shot-shells, and bullets offered by this firm. Below the cartridge display are 5 mounted cartridge box labels. It measures 35" x 40" and sold at auction for $17,925.

This German strongbow circa 1600 is made of iron with braided, tarred hemp string. The finely carved walnut butt has inlays and additions made from bone and is engraved with a coat of arms and various depictions of animals. It measures 22" l and sold at auction for $3,500.

An 18th century European combination hunting sword flintlock pistol sword with unique decoration, gooseneck hammer centrally hung from the back of the sword handle which contains the lock, sword blade smooth and light gray, a rare firearms curiosity and most rare with the depiction of a Native American, 21" overall, with 5" octagon to round barrel .38 caliber pistol attached to the right side of the blade, $3,585. Gamers might recognize this weapon as the Gunblades from the *Final Fantasy* series, which began with *Final Fantasy VIII* as the iconic weapon of Squall Leonhart.

This collection of four English silver trophy cups are dated from 1855 to 1930 and measure 10" h and tip in at 69 oz of silver. Including examples from the Aberdeenshire Coursing Club in 1855 to The Rothschild Stag Hounds Puppy Cup, a military challenge bowl, the trophies come from the extensive eclectic collection of Malcolm S. Forbes and sold at auction for $2,390.

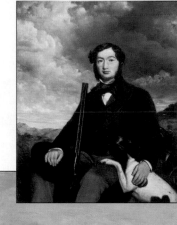

Gentleman with a Hunting Dog before an Extensive Landscape, oil on canvas, 50-1/4" x 40", $2,987.

This Southern German baroque mirror with hunting-theme décor dates to 1740. Measuring roughly 30" x 30", the frame sold at auction for $3,500.

A superb hunting subject, this 1943 original calendar art by Edgar Franklin Whitmack was published as a popular calendar print by the Osbourne Calendar Company. Rendered in oil on board, it has an approximate sight size of 12" x 17-1/2" and sold at auction for $1,610.

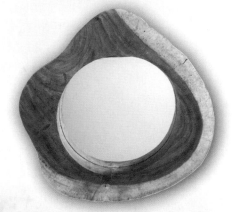

A hunting-themed still life by Marie V. Valenzi, 1877, oil on canvas, 26" x 35", $3,700.

A cool tree trunk framed mirror, 22" x 22", sold at auction for $281.

Produced circa 1858, this rare prototype J. Rider experimental revolver is equipped with a unique trigger guard-loading lever. The plunger is housed in the lower frame and is attached to the upper front of the trigger guard, and the rear of the trigger guard latches into the frame directly behind the trigger; when pushed forward, the trigger guard unhooks and can swing down to work the plunger. It sold at auction for $4,182.

CHAPTER
12

DANGEROUS PURSUIT

GUNS AND KNIVES

Collecting dangerous weaponry is a lot like spending thousands of dollars for a work of art that can also be used to protect your family from a zombie apocalypse. But that's generally not the primary reason collectors look for new and unusual weapons. The most desirable and valuable examples are often made so because of strong historical importance, whether through a mechanical innovation, provenance, or high design. Sometimes all three come together to create, well, a very bad idea. These oddities, one-offs or outright "failures" are often the most valuable and sought after weapons of all. Take, for example, the case of the Philippine Guerrilla Gun.

The gun was designed by Iliff D. "Rich" Richardson (a manlier name there wasn't), a former executive officer of Motor Torpedo Boat PT-34. When the Japanese sunk his boat in 1942, Richardson took up with a group of guerilla forces to defend the Philippine islands. He lived the gritty guerilla fighter life and was taught how to fend off enemy forces with very basic weaponry. We're talking one step up from gunpowder charged slingshots. After he returned stateside, Richardson's manly memoirs served as the basis for a book and movie titled,

In 1946, you could have owned a brand new Philippine Guerilla Gun that had all the technology of hitting a shotgun shell with a nail and hammer.

An American Guerilla in the Philippines. His movie featured heroic battle scenes fending off enemy forces MacGuyver-style, with a crude single-shot "slam-fire" action 12-gauge shotgun. These guns are the firearm equivalent to prison hooch: The entire weapon only has five parts and has no trigger, no hammer, no extractor, no magazine, no sights, and no choke tubes. The gun is loaded by removing the barrel and dropping a shell into the breech end. The barrel is replaced and then fired by quickly pushing the barrel forward and then jerking it back, striking the shell against a firing pin fixed to the breechblock. In all honesty, the shotguns look like something a teenager could make in a dystopian woodshop.

After the movie's success, Richardson tried to parlay his newfound fame into a commercial venture to actually sell these jungle shotguns to American consumers and in 1946 began producing the Model R5 Philippine Guerrilla Gun under the name Richardson Industries of East Haven, Conn. Once it hit the market, it was an absolute failure, but not for the reason you might expect: Safety wasn't the primary concern among consumers, but rather the primitive nature didn't appeal to hunters who could easily afford a better quality (not to mention far more accurate) small-gauge game gun. However, when these guns appear at auction, they now fetch about $300 to $400—or about the same cost as a new base brand shotgun.

Now that's the target for a Dangerous Pursuit. Collectors of antique guns are hardcore history buffs and love shooting. The people who collect knives are fascinated by a craftsman's ability to turn a dull chunk of steel into a gleaming and functional work of art. The fact that items can be used to cause great bodily harm is secondary to their design, their place in history, and how well the technology carried out its intent.

MANTIQUES FACT

During World War II, President Franklin D. Roosevelt commissioned the Office of Strategic Services to head up foreign intelligence services but the agency was also responsible for developing spy gadgets ranging from silenced pistols to 16mm Kodak cameras in the shape of a matchbox to something called "Aunt Jemima," an allegedly explosive powder packaged in Chinese flour bags.

If the key to anything you own can double as a pistol, it must be pretty valuable or you've hit a new level on the Paranoid Meter. This is an example of an extremely rare percussion combination key/pistol. Measuring 4-1/2" in total length, the underside of the barrel is fitted with a 7/8" long key bit, marked "677" on the left side. The right side of the frame near the breech marked "BREVETE SGLG/ ED." Grips are smooth bag-shaped ivory. It sold at auction for $2,750.

This miniature Thompson Model 1928 sub-machine gun measures 15-1/2" overall, with a blue finish, fluted barrel, detachable magazine, and shoulder stock. Simulates open bolt operation, with functional safety, but the barrel is not bored through. It sold at auction for $2,000.

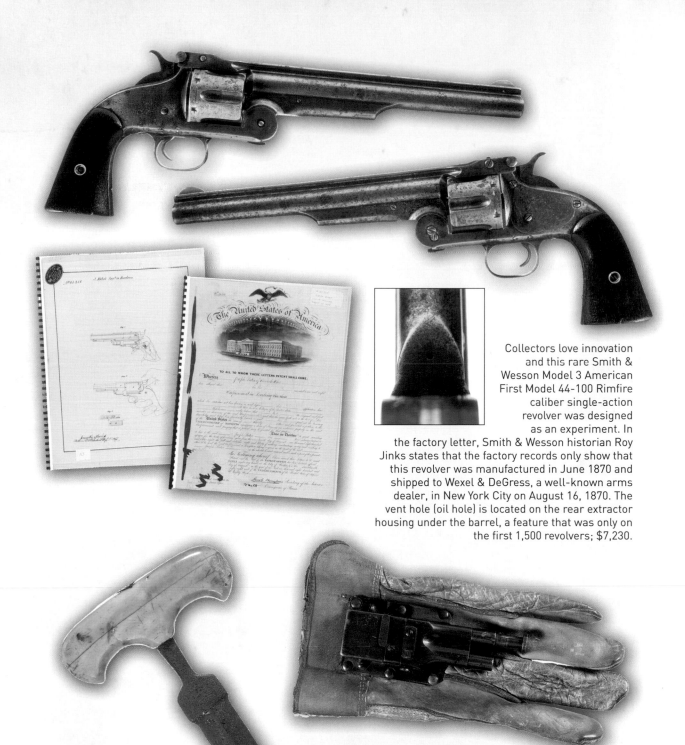

Collectors love innovation and this rare Smith & Wesson Model 3 American First Model 44-100 Rimfire caliber single-action revolver was designed as an experiment. In the factory letter, Smith & Wesson historian Roy Jinks states that the factory records only show that this revolver was manufactured in June 1870 and shipped to Wexel & DeGress, a well-known arms dealer, in New York City on August 16, 1870. The vent hole (oil hole) is located on the rear extractor housing under the barrel, a feature that was only on the first 1,500 revolvers; $7,230.

Alternately known as a push knife, fist knife, push dirk, or T-handled knife, this push dagger has a "T"-bone handle designed to be grasped in the hand so that the blade protrudes from the front of one's fist, typically between the 2nd and 3rd finger. The dagger shown here may have been made by Will & Finck of San Francisco, Calif., but any maker markings are long gone due to extensive aging or rust ... or blood? The blade measures 3-1/8" l and it sold at auction for $2,185.

Representing the complete opposite of a handshake, the Sedgley Fist Gun was developed by a Stanley M. Height on behalf of the U.S. Navy, which filed a patent application for the gun on February 29, 1944. Evidently, the weapon was used by specially trained personnel during WWII. It consists of a .38 Smith & Wesson smoothbore barrel with superposed trigger mechanism, swivel breech, and sliding safety. The gun is attached to a leather glove with six brass rivets. When the shooter forms a fist, the push trigger is exposed and the gun fires when the trigger makes contact with the target. The gun has a blue finish. The mounting plate is roll-stamped with the markings: "HAND FIRING/MECHANISM-MK-2" over the encircled "S" Sedgley logo, $8,625.

Manufactured around 1870 (possibly in Belgium), this umbrella has a bamboo shaft and silver hardware with an iron tip. But wait, there's more! When the horn handle is rotated slightly to the left, it quickly releases a pepperbox pistol/dagger combo! BAM! Now who's got blue eyes cryin' in the rain? It sold at auction for $3,450.

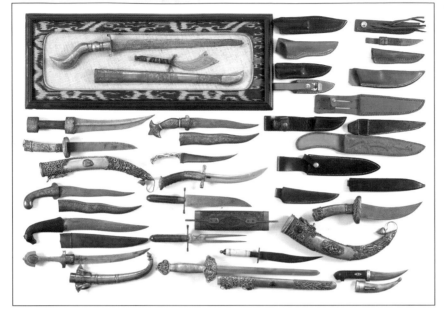

Knives are a popular collectible and this group represents the most common bladesto collect. Shown here are 19 various knives and daggers, chiefly Middle Eastern or Indian in origin, some showing fine Damascus blades and silver decoration, and leather sheaths. The whole collection sold at auction for $920.

This grouping represents the tools of the trade of the buffalo market hunter active in the 1870s. The entire kit was carried from hunt to hunt in a wagon and only removed when in the immediate vicinity of the herd. It features a Sharps Model 1874 Old Reliable Sporting Rifle with the original buffalo fur-covered traveling box and related accoutrements. It sold at auction for $19,550.

Produced by Colt at an unknown date, this 22 cal. "Space Age" target pistol is ergonomically excellent while featuring a futuristic design. The mechanism is unique in Colt's auto-pistols, with a detachable blue polymer tube magazine feeding from the left side, with a rear cocking knob, heavy bull barrel, Patridge front and adjustable rear sights. It sold at auction for $5,500.

A very cool invention, this pocketknife is of all-steel construction, with smooth side panels and a 2-3/4" clip point knife blade. Running alongside the folded blade is a pistol barrel, marked "PATENTED" on top, with the trigger on the underside. Measuring 6-1/2" in overall length with the blade open, $1,725.

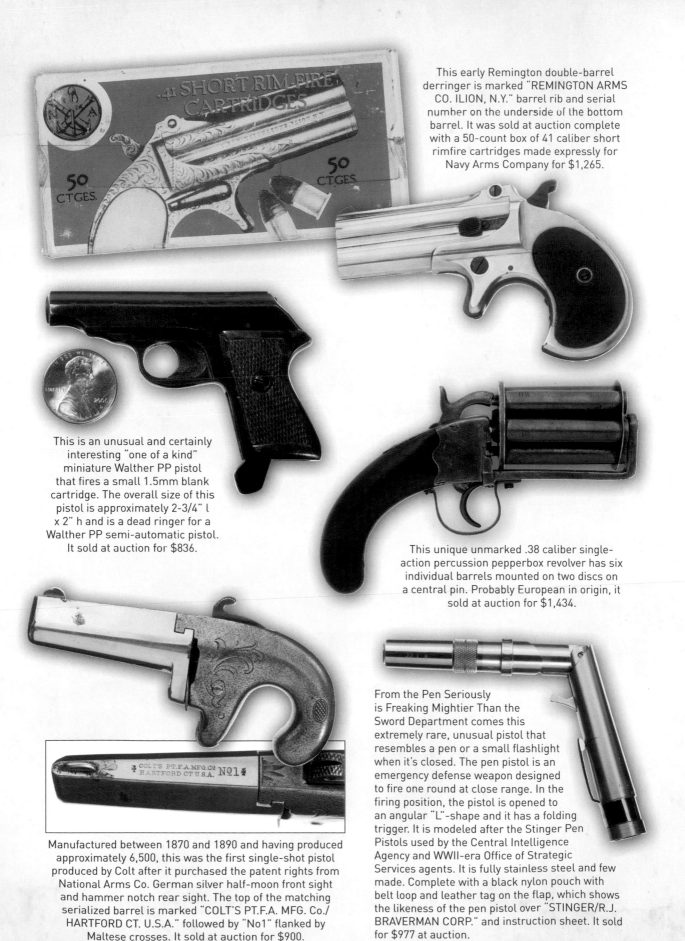

This early Remington double-barrel derringer is marked "REMINGTON ARMS CO. ILION, N.Y." barrel rib and serial number on the underside of the bottom barrel. It was sold at auction complete with a 50-count box of 41 caliber short rimfire cartridges made expressly for Navy Arms Company for $1,265.

This is an unusual and certainly interesting "one of a kind" miniature Walther PP pistol that fires a small 1.5mm blank cartridge. The overall size of this pistol is approximately 2-3/4" l x 2" h and is a dead ringer for a Walther PP semi-automatic pistol. It sold at auction for $836.

This unique unmarked .38 caliber single-action percussion pepperbox revolver has six individual barrels mounted on two discs on a central pin. Probably European in origin, it sold at auction for $1,434.

Manufactured between 1870 and 1890 and having produced approximately 6,500, this was the first single-shot pistol produced by Colt after it purchased the patent rights from National Arms Co. German silver half-moon front sight and hammer notch rear sight. The top of the matching serialized barrel is marked "COLT'S PT.F.A. MFG. Co./ HARTFORD CT. U.S.A." followed by "No1" flanked by Maltese crosses. It sold at auction for $900.

From the Pen Seriously is Freaking Mightier Than the Sword Department comes this extremely rare, unusual pistol that resembles a pen or a small flashlight when it's closed. The pen pistol is an emergency defense weapon designed to fire one round at close range. In the firing position, the pistol is opened to an angular "L"-shape and it has a folding trigger. It is modeled after the Stinger Pen Pistols used by the Central Intelligence Agency and WWII-era Office of Strategic Services agents. It is fully stainless steel and few made. Complete with a black nylon pouch with belt loop and leather tag on the flap, which shows the likeness of the pen pistol over "STINGER/R.J. BRAVERMAN CORP." and instruction sheet. It sold for $977 at auction.

CHAPTER
13

ROCK AND REMEMBER
MUSIC MEMORABILIA

About the time Bob Wingate turned 40, he decided he was ready to sell the electric guitar he had kept since his teens.

He figured the best place to find a buyer was at a massive guitar show held nearby just a few times a year. Walking through the show brought wave after wave of memories: his first guitar from Honest Joe's Pawn Shop, garage rock bands, driving around Dallas with Jimmy and Stevie Ray Vaughn. "It was just amazing, the memories that came back," he says.

OPPOSITE PAGE: Sitting by his Wurlitzer Bubbler Jukebox, Bob holds a 1956 Gretsch Chet Atkins 6120, known to collectors as the "Cow & Cactus" Model.

RIGHT: A 1956 Gibson ES-350T, just like the one Chuck Berry played in the mid-to-late 1950s.

Despite this, Bob still found a buyer for his old guitar. On the way home from the show, he called his wife. "Well, did you buy another one?" she asked. That was all he needed to hear. "I slammed on the brakes and did a U-turn," Bob says.

That was about 25 years ago and Bob's collection has grown to more than 20 instruments and a wall full of authentic concert posters, gold records and memorabilia, and 12 gigs a month in his own band.

"If you go back and play these old instruments," Bob says, "they sound just like the sounds of their era. The jazz bass sounds like a 1930s dive. Everything's got a story."

Take, for instance, the 1946 Wurlitzer 1015 Bubbler Jukebox in the corner of his music room.

Bob picked it up for about $175 when he was 18 and restored it from a shambling mess to a gleaming beacon of rock 'n' roll.

The juke stands guard over a parade of the very best from what Bob calls the golden age of electric guitars, those made between 1955 and 1965. Special examples include a 1958 Gibson ES-350-T natural semi-hollow acoustic electric, a 1956 Gretsch Round Up amplifier in its original tooled leather, and a 1960 Gibson ES-330 natural. There's also the Gibson Les Paul TV Model from '56 and a Thin-line Gibson from 1959.

Like many smart collectors, he bought the best he could afford at the time and made good use of shows and dealers and the early days of eBay. He bought and sold and traded up. "I wish I bought more in the early 1990s," he says.

The growing collection rekindled his passion for playing music. In his 50s, when most guys have one foot in retirement, Bob

The 1946 Wurlitzer 1015 Bubbler Jukebox Bob restored when he was 18. It survived many moves and still plays 45s from his collection.

Bob Wingate's music room is a place to remember and a place to practice for the next gig.

Bob puts his 1937 Kay Upright Bass and a rare, 1929 National Guitar Tri-Cone Resonator on display next to his collection of blues artist posters.

figured it was an ideal time to learn the drums. He connected with a friend and formed The Tu-Tones, a two-man band that performs about 12 gigs a month at bars and events. They recently released a CD and it's pretty darn good.

For Bob, his collection is more about making the most of the time you've got left to live than it is about making just another purchase.

"You've got to do something," he says. "You've got to do something other than sitting by the pool all day."

Bob's love for 1960s California Surf music led to the design of his custom Stratocaster Surf Guitar made by Fender's Master Guitar Builder John English in the mid-'90s.

In 2004, Fender produced only 100 Stevie Ray Vaughan (SRV) Tribute Stratocasters. Fender's Master builder John Cruz worked closely with Jimmie Vaughan to photograph and compile exact measurements of Stevie's "Numbero Uno" to produce this awesome Strat.

A stunning and beautifully hand-engraved 1935 National Tri-Cone Resonator Lap Style guitar made specifically for playing Hawaiian music.

Collectors know this 1953 Fender Telecaster as the "Blackguard Tele."

Known as the new Les Paul, this 1961 Gibson SG Standard sports a sideways Vibrola Tailpiece.

Thousands of guitarists learned how to play in the late '50s on guitars like Gibson's famous 1959 Les Paul Junior.

$266,500

$26,250

A classic from the high point of rock, this 1962 Fender Stratocaster electric guitar in fiesta red sold for $26,250 at auction.

$10,175

This first year production 1963 Gibson Firebird III Sunburst electric guitar sold for $10,175.

A 1949 Bigsby Birdseye Maple Solid Body Electric Guitar, #51649, completed May 16, 1949, sold at auction for $266,500. It was designed by Paul Bigsby (1899-1968), best known as the creator of the first successful vibrato tailpiece (or "whammy bar" as it's often called) for the electric guitar.

$5,000

Scott Ian, lead guitarist for the thrash metal band Anthrax, was the first to bring his passion for horror movies and comic books to his performances. A Washburn Murder Weapon V guitar Ian used on tour and in the studio (splattered with fake blood) sold at auction for $5,000.

This John Lennon-themed Rickenbacker guitar (No. 1,536 of 2,000) was designed by Greg Rich, who is considered by many to be the creator of "art guitars." It sold at auction for $17,925.

Not only is this one of only two known examples of a Mark V-style Mosrite Gospel model guitar, this is Kurt Cobain's Mosrite Gospel model guitar. While Cobain owned and smashed many cheaper (usually Univox) copies of Mosrite guitars during his career, this was one of the two Mosrites he owned. It was modified for Cobain with a strap button added to the treble side horn, and the original metal string guide has been flipped to allow it to be strung left handed. The original case bears the words "NIRVANA" and "F**k Elvis" (expletive deleted). It sold at auction for $131,450.

This rattlesnake guitar strap owned by Rudy Sarzo, who played with White Snake, Quiet Riot, Ozzy Osborne and Dio, symbolizes the transition years of 1983-85 when music focused as much on its image as it did its music with the arrival of heavy metal and hairbands. The strap sold for $400 at auction.

A 1981 concert poster and the original preliminary art by Rick Griffin to promote the Grateful Dead *Reckoning* album, $5,937.

A Batman-inspired first printing BG-2 Fillmore Series poster for Big Brother and the Holding Company performance from 1966, $7,170.

It seems popularity for all things Beatles will never grow old and this poster for their 1966 performance at Candlestick Park sold for $5,975 at auction.

A classic Beatles at Shea Stadium concert poster sold at auction for $11,250.

134   **MANTIQUES** *A Manly Guide to Cool Stuff*

Iron Maiden with Rock Goddess concert poster, Belgium, original logo to market to both Dutch and French fans, 1983, $100.

A 1967 circular poster promoting The Doors at the Kaleidoscope Club, $11,875.

CASTING CALL FOR NIRVANA FANS!!!

NIRVANA

needs YOU to appear in their upcoming music video, Smells Like Teen Spirit. You should be 18 to 25 years old and adapt a high-school personna, i.e., preppy, punk, nerd, jock... No clothing with name brands or logos please! You will need to be at GMT Studios, Stage 6 on SATURDAY AUGUST 17 at 11:30 a.m. Be prepared to stay for several hours! Come support Nirvana and have a great time!

GMT
5721 Buckingham Pky.
Culver City, CA
(213) 649-3733

Most all of the kids who appear in Nirvana's music video for "Smells Like Teen Spirit" are the same fans who attended a concert at the Roxey at Sunset Boulevard in Hollywood the night before. They were handed this casting flier before they went home. Few remain, probably because the flier was printed on 11" by 17" paper. The fact this survived is a collecting miracle and explains its $1,500 sale price at auction.

Pasadena, Calif., was ground zero for hot bands in the mid-1970s. Bands would often play backyard parties along the Southern California coast and this handbill announcing an up-and-coming group called Van Halen is valued at $300 to $500.

An awesome 1970 BG-222 Filmore Series concert poster promoted by Bill Graham featuring Jefferson Airplane sold at auction for $9,560.

Few posters are as iconic as this 1968 Bill Graham "Flying Eyeball" Fillmore/Winterland BG-105 Filmore Series poster promoting the Jimi Hendrix Experience. It sold at auction for $9,560.

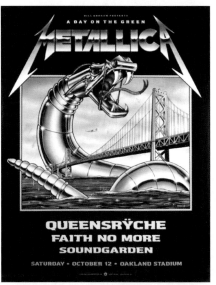

Metallica poster, San Francisco, 1991, Bill Graham Presents, $250.

MANTIQUES FACT

Bill Graham remains the most significant and relevant concert promoter of all time and did more than just organize or promote concerts—he is credited with establishing music as a crucial part of pop culture. Graham's posters were among the first collected in 1966 and his original concert series in Filmore, N.Y., and in Filmore West and Winterland in San Francisco set a standard by which all others are judged. Graham's numbered concert poster series is referred to by collectors as "The Filmore Series of 289 posters." A second series of Graham posters are harder to find because they weren't necessarily tied to a specific venue.

Slayer concert poster, Belgium, circa 1990s, $50.

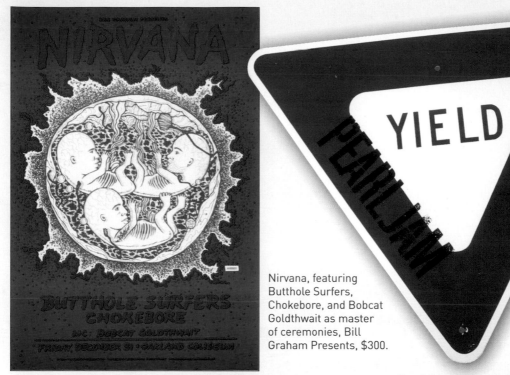

Nirvana, featuring Butthole Surfers, Chokebore, and Bobcat Goldthwait as master of ceremonies, Bill Graham Presents, $300.

Pearl Jam promo sign, Epic Records, obnoxious sheet metal sign to promote the group's fifth studio album, *Yield*, $200.

This press book produced in 1980 for Black Sabbath sold for $50 at auction.

A cool Bill Graham poster promoting the 1966 concert for The Wailers sold at auction for $133.

Black plastic finger pick from Buddy Holly's personal belongings, $2,778.

Slayer guitar picks from the June 22, 2010 concert The Big Four: Live from Sofia, Bulgaria, featuring Metallica, Slayer, Megadeth, and Anthrax, are valued from $150 to $200 each.

Metallica guitar picks, 2010, $50 each.

There is something inherently cool about seeing a wall of Marshall speakers in front of you at a concert and although this amplifier cabinet doesn't look like much, it holds a prominent place in rock history: It once composed the tower of noise, shown behind Ace Frehley, that was a trademark of KISS' 1974-76 concert tour; $4,500.

Van Halen could well be credited as the first band to introduce thousands of screaming fans to beach balls at concerts. During the group's final show of the Van Halen II Tour in Los Angeles on Oct. 7, 1979, singer David Lee Roth fired these balls into the crowd. One sold at auction for $200.

Vintage Rock T-Shirts

It's time to stop buying T-shirts in a bag. You can easily find vintage rock 'n' roll concert and commemorative shirts in themed auctions and at music shows. Prices start as low as $20 to $30 for an original 1980s or 1990s vintage shirt.

The more valuable shirts usually have some historical tie to the group. Members of Metallica designed the band's first concert T-shirt as a premium for buying the group's demo, *No Life 'til Leather*. It sold for $1,500 at auction. The demo was released in 1982 and 30 years later, the shirts are impossible to find.

Early shirts promoting *Method of Destruction* sell for as much as $800 and those featuring Anthrax and other heavy metal groups can be found from $100 to $1,000.

FREE SWEAT STAINS! Crosby, Stills, Nash & Young was one of the last acts to play during the legendary Woodstock Music & Art Fair, taking the stage around 3 a.m. This is Graham Nash's T-shirt from that historical concert, which sold at auction for $896.

Judas Priest promotional T-shirt, Columbia Records, a relic from the founding fathers of British heavy metal, $75.

Cool Elvis Presley 1956 T-shirt, a child's size 16-18 or medium, sold at auction for $375.

Kurt Cobain wore this shirt on at least two important occasions at the height of Nirvana's popularity. On January 2, 1992, *Nevermind* reached #1 on Billboard's Top Albums chart, and just days later, Nirvana taped a live performance at MTV Studios, where Cobain is first photographed wearing the "Punk Rock Duck" shirt. A few weeks later, he again wore the shirt, now modified with a hand-drawn message, "Kill the Grateful Dead," in an attempt to derail an important photo shoot with *Rolling Stone* for the magazine's cover. Cobain actually brought two shirts to the *Rolling Stone* shoot in Australia in February 1992, and both were photographed. Cobain proved a difficult subject, refusing to remove his sunglasses in several of the shots. Surprisingly, the magazine chose a photo of the shirt that was customized by Cobain with the message, "Corporate Magazines Still Suck," rather than the Punk Rock Duck shirt, and the published cover became iconic. The set (along with a group of Nirvana memorabilia) sold at auction for $7,500.

With kick-ass Victorian-era lithography and portraiture featuring an intriguing assortment of 19th century sporting legends, the N28 Allen & Ginter "The World's Champions" set is considered one of the true masterpieces of the early trading card hobby. Among the baseball stars pictured are eventual Cooperstown fixtures Cap Anson, John Clarkson, Charles Comiskey, Tim Keefe, Mike "King" Kelly, and John Ward. John L. Sullivan anchors the roster of bare-knuckle pugilists, while "Buffalo Bill" Cody and Annie Oakley provide firepower for the gun enthusiast. Rowers, wrestlers, and billiards players help to round out the cast of fifty names. It sold at auction for $478.

Look at this man. This is a man who wants to play ball, not take your crap; 1916 photo of Babe Ruth as a member of the Boston Red Sox, $17,925.

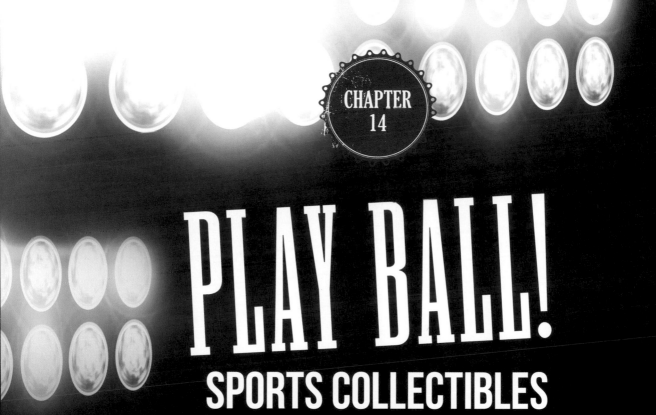

CHAPTER 14

PLAY BALL!

SPORTS COLLECTIBLES

Gary Seidenfrau collects the stuff of true legends.

His home office has a desk, but the walls are covered with signed baseballs, bats, and black and white photos. The room is a shrine to the men who not only played professional sports, but used the games to build something in their lives.

"Mantle. Musial. DiMaggio. Mays. Aaron. They're all there on probably 150 bats and 200 to 300 balls," he says. "I don't chase after the young guys. I'm always going after the guys who were the real heroes."

His collection soon overtook the study and spilled over into his son's bedroom and elsewhere in his house.

There's only been a few times when Gary has been knocked out of the running for a special item. He still remembers the seven-day auction of his friend Barry Halper's epic baseball memorabilia collection. The September 1999 auction held by Sotheby's in New York still stands as one of the most important collections ever offered by a single private owner. The 2,481-lot auction grossed more than $21.8 million, as every single piece in the collection found a new owner with 85 percent of the collection selling above its high estimate.

"By the time I raised my paddle off my lap to the middle of my chest–before I could get it all the way up–the bidding took things past $3,000, $4,000, $5,000. It was incredible. Then the Mantle glove comes up."

Gary watched as the floor bidding for Mickey Mantle's circa 1960 game-used glove blew past its $20,000 high estimate only to stall out at $100,000. "Then a phone bidder got involved but all of us were watching Billy Crystal up in a skybox. It kept going up and up and up and Billy kept bidding. Every

One of Gary's favorite collections is made up of more than 60 boxing gloves signed by fighters inducted to the Boxing Hall of Fame over the last decade.

Gary Seidenfrau collects true sports legends.

time he bid, his knees would sink lower and lower until it was all over—$239,000!"

Reports at the time said Crystal emerged from the skybox to shout a quip at the auctioneer: "Can I jump from here?"

His collections don't stop with baseball heroes. One of his favorite collections is made up of more than 60 boxing gloves signed by fighters inducted to the Boxing Hall of Fame over the last decade.

"When you meet them, you see how down to earth they are," he says. "No pretense. Real guys. They fought in the streets and a lot of them worked their way up out of underprivileged neighborhoods. Some got taken advantage of over the years but some of them made it huge."

The glove collection was inspired by a childhood spent boxing in Brooklyn, N.Y., and watching matches on Friday Night Fights with his dad. The collection came together over the past 10 years of attending special events for inductees to the Boxing Hall of Fame in Canastota, N.Y. Once a year, Gary and his wife make a special trip to meet up with friends and spend a weekend of talking boxing and meeting the fighters. Gloves signed by Roberto Duran, Ken Norton, Larry Holmes, and Lennox Lewis hang in a row in his rec room. His favorite still stands as the best boxer of all time. "He signed it Muhammad Ali aka Cassius Clay," Gary says.

Gary's collection is less about the stuff than it is about the experiences he's shared with friends and family. His best experiences were being with his family at Yankees Stadium, especially at the '96, '98, '99, and 2000 World Series. He's a supporter of the Baseball Hall of Fame, a former Yankees season ticket holder, and was a close friend to Al Marchfled, a fixture at Madison

Square Garden for more than 60 years up until Marchfeld passed away in September 2013. The two had much in common: Hard-working guys from humble backgrounds who shared a deep, steadfast love for New York's greatest sports heroes. Marchfeld's stories of working for the Brooklyn Dodgers and the New York Knicks since the late 1940s are legendary. "He told me about the time when he was a batboy for the Dodgers. Leo Durocher, the manager, asked him to walk down to the train station to pick up the new rookie but they didn't tell him the guy's name. 'How am I going to know who the new guy is?' Marchfled asked.

"Durocher told him: 'You'll know him when you see him. He's black.' They sent Al down to pick up Jackie Robinson."

Without a doubt, this is the finest baseball machine ever produced by any company and is a must have for a collector of arcade machines, as well as those who are baseball collectors. Featured are the infamous baseball players of the 1937 World Series games such as DiMaggio, Gehrig, Dickey, Chapman, etc. at bat and in the outfield Medwick, Dykes, Dean, Averill, etc. After a coin is deposited, a ball appears from the umpire's chest (standing behind pitcher) and hands off the ball to the pitcher. The pitcher then throws the ball to you in one of a variety of pitches, and you swing your bat. The accurate system of balls and strikes is kept by means of steel balls in marked troughs. Many options can occur such as hitting directly to the shortstop for an out, down the 1st or 3rd base line for a home run, a foul ball, double, or a direct shot to Dizzy Dean, the pitcher, for an out. All the while the three outfielders, as well as the four infielders, are nervously twitching and moving slightly from left to right, positioning themselves and awaiting to see your mastery at bat. The game is 40" w x 54" h x 29-1/2" d and sold at auction for $33,350.

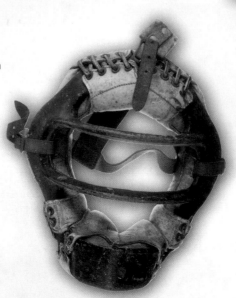

This is one of just a few known surviving catcher's masks worn by Hall of Famer backstop Yogi Berra during his Yankees tenure. It appears practically medieval in its construction, with a black cast iron shell to which soft padded brown leather is strapped with leather bands. Catcher's gear from this iconic Yankee is the toughest of quarry for the Yankee collector, $16,730.

What appears to be a rubber squeeze toy for a pet, this Cleveland Indians mascot piece was issued circa 1940s, and is a 6-1/2" rarity. It sold for $54 at auction.

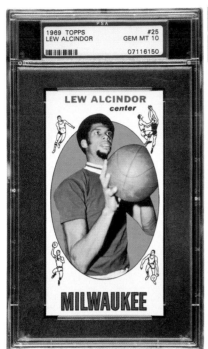

$209,125

The 99-card series is the cornerstone of any advanced basketball collection. The roster features twenty-five Hall of Famers including Jerry West, Oscar Robertson, and Wilt Chamberlain, with the rookie cards of Lew Alcindor (Kareem Abdul-Jabbar), John Havlicek, Bill Bradley, Wes Unseld, and others. It was the first comprehensive basketball edition in eight years and the first Topps basketball release since 1957, $209,125.

$717,000

$41,825

Much like the man it celebrates, this card will establish its new owner as the top dog in the Michael Jordan card market, as the BGS 9.5 rating is both unsurpassed and unequalled. More examples of Jordan's essential 1985-86 Fleer rookie card have graded PSA Gem Mint 10 (140, to be exact) than the entire population of the offered lot. Exceedingly rare in any state, $41,825.

This is the jersey Lou Gehrig was wearing when the Yankees dominated in 1927. With a batting order called Murderer's Row for obvious reasons, the team delivered the most devastating three-four punch for its historical context that the game has ever seen. Ruth's sixty circuits in 1927 was trailed by Gehrig's forty-seven. In fact, the duo of Ruth and Gehrig produced more than twice the home run output of every other American League team, with the exception of the Philadelphia Athletics, who just avoided being doubled with fifty-six; $717,000.

5 Collectibles That Show Why Babe Ruth Will Always Be the Badass of Baseball

Babe Ruth changed baseball forever. He shook up the epic snooze-fest the game had become in the 1920s through sheer kick-ass athletic prowess and a love of the game. Or was it for the love of free beer and hot dogs? Either way, fans today can draw a straight line from Ruth's accomplishments to today's sports traditions. The following Babe Ruth mantiques represent points in his career that changed the game for good.

The finest Babe Ruth single-signed baseball known. Any great sports memorabilia collection should include a signed baseball. They aren't hard to find, partly because Ruth was among the first to see his autograph meant big money for his fans. Ruth's own granddaughter once admitted The Bambino would sign bats and balls all winter long and store them in a barn in preparation for "the busy season." He signed balls by the hundreds for the poor kids living around Yankee Stadium because he knew they were selling them to keep their family fed during the Great Depression. That said, collectors zero in on the best examples. This one is considered the finest Babe Ruth signed baseball known to exist, which helps explain why it brought a whopping $388,375 at auction.

Babe Ruth 1933 All-Star Game-worn jersey. Fit for either the Smithsonian Institution or the Baseball Hall of Fame, Babe Ruth's #3 New York Yankees jersey remains a shining symbol of pre-war Americana. When he wore this jersey during Major League Baseball's very first All-Star Game, Ruth was at the height of his appetites for wine, women, and song. Although it marked the beginning of his slide into retirement and his struggle with weight, the year was still a career standout as he batted .301, with 34 home runs, 103 RBIs, and a league-leading 114 walks. His jersey sold for a whopping $657,250.

Circa 1932 Babe Ruth game-worn New York Yankees cap. The perfect complement to your Ruth-signed ball is one of his game-worn New York Yankee caps. This cap dates to 1932, the year his called shot during the fifth inning of Game 3 of the World Series gave him permanent status as stone cold awesome. Yes, Ruth was quite the showman and his penchant for antics on the field filled seats like few others could. His cap sold for $200,000 at auction.

1933 Goudey Big League Triple Babe Ruth uncut sheet. The 1933 Goudey Gum series of 240 was produced by the Boston-based Goudey Gum manufacturer in ten sheets containing 24 cards each, which were then cut, packaged with a stick of gum, and distributed. Naturally, Babe's famous chubby puss would grace what is now considered the first major gum card set of the 1930s. It sold at auction for $131,450.

1916 M101-5 blank back Babe Ruth rookie card. From his humble beginnings from an orphanage in a poor section of Baltimore, Ruth's rookie card was released when he was fresh-faced 21 years old. His "rags to riches" story represents the best of The American Dream. A single 1916 M101-5 Blank Back Babe Ruth Rookie card #151 sold for $101,575 at auction.

The most significant trading card find in hobby history emerged from a small Ohio town, discovered in an attic in a box long forgotten. The pristine relics from the Dead Ball Era made their debut more than 100 years later – in 2012. Of the thirty players from the E98 series, the collection offered twenty-five players in two color variations, and a trio represented by a single background. The roster includes the greatest of the game including Ty Cobb, Honus Wagner, Chief Bender, Christy Mathewson, Connie Mack, Frank Chance, Hughie Jennings, Johnny Evers, Roger Bresnahan, Cy Young plus others. $286,800

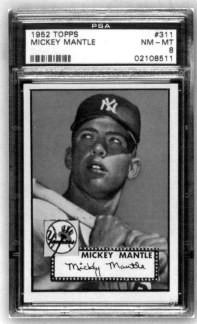

The image on this 1952 Topps Mickey Mantle card is an American icon, with the Mick posed in a right-handed batting stance, his eyes drifting up to the grandstand behind him, $77,675.

In a gutsy performance reminiscent of Roy Hobbs' climactic scene from *The Natural*, a wounded Curt Schilling ignored the advice of the physician who had pieced back together the ragged tendons of his right ankle and took to the mound, first in a crucial Game Six to stave off American League Championship Series elimination against the hated New York Yankees, and then again in Game Two of the World Series to claim the second victory in a four-game sweep of the St. Louis Cardinals. In each television broadcast, the cameras repeatedly locked onto the growing red stain at Schilling's sutured push-off ankle, as the star right-hander battled to victory over two elite batting line-ups and his own remarkable threshold for pain. By the time the Sox had completed their extraordinary eight-game run to turn the tide from a three-game ALCS deficit to a World Series sweep, the Bloody Sock was firmly implanted in American sports history as the main prop of a script too unbelievable for any Hollywood screenwriter, $92,612.

While a limited original print run owns the blame for Honus Wagner's intense scarcity today, the debate over the cause for this quick cessation remains a century later, although historians agree it was Wagner himself who pulled the plug, denying the use of his image in what would become the hobby's most popular tobacco issue. The most popular story explaining his refusal is that Wagner wished to play no role in the promotion of the use of tobacco, though it has been stated that he was himself a user and had appeared in advertisements for many tobacco products previously. Another theory notes Wagner's reputation as a fierce negotiator, arguing that it was nothing more than a case cash that led the American Tobacco Company to end production of Wagner's card almost as soon as it started; $262,900.

An unopened 1973 Topps Baseball Series 4 wax pack box with 24 uncirculated packs still contained inside the close to mint condition box they have called home since 1973. This series contained stars and HoFers Gaylord Perry, Willie McCovey, Juan Marichal, and Phil Niekro, plus various teams/coaches, along with the ever popular "All-Time Leader" cards, $2,987.

This large collection of early boxing photos sold at auction for $150.

If only the Red Sox had this many pennants. The work of one Fenway fanatic is compiled into a single auction lot, $215.

1971 Panini Olympia unopened pack, with Cassius Clay on back of pack, GAI Gem Mint 9.5. Cassius Clay's "B" issue can be seen through the Minty yellow wrapper on this unopened pack of 1971 Panini Olympia cards. Graded an impressive GAI 9.5 Gem Mint, this piece will fit best in any serious Ali hobbyists' collections; $101.

These are the white satin Everlast trunks worn by Muhammad Ali as he inflicted and endured the most brutal beatings ever witnessed in a Heavyweight Championship bout against Joe Frazier, known as the "Thrilla in Manilla." Written in black marker on the front is: "Ali - Frazier Fight, Trilla (sic) in Manila, Pres. F. Marcos, Manila, Philippines, Oct. 1, 1975." $155,350.

Any fortunate football die-hard who has ever set foot in Fuzzy Thurston's bar on Mason Street in Green Bay understands the magic and utter nostalgia of this helmet, worn by one of the most beloved Green Bay Packer players and Packer Hall of Famer during the Vince Lombardi era; $6,572.

This set of 10 rare American College Football Premiums from 1950 is $100–$200.

Modern American football is the offspring of various forms of a sport that has its origins dating back to medieval Europe. This series is hard to complete and few sets are ever made available at public auction; $35,850.

To the current standard of football protective headgear, we have to say, you've come a long way, baby. This turn-of-the-century football nose mask was the cutting edge of early gridiron armor, essentially a heavy rubber shield that covers the nose, and is held in place by a cloth strap and a molded "bite plate" that fit between the teeth. Ancient teeth marks are still clearly visible from its days of use; $15,535.

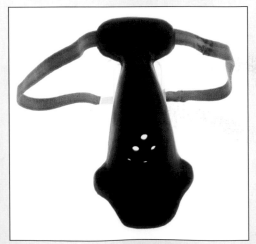

This 1980 USA Olympic hockey jersey worn by Mike Eruzione during "The Miracle on Ice" game is a treasure not only amongst sports memorabilia, but American history; $657,250.

A collection of six mantique golf clubs in a shadowbox sold for $325 at an auction in Houston.

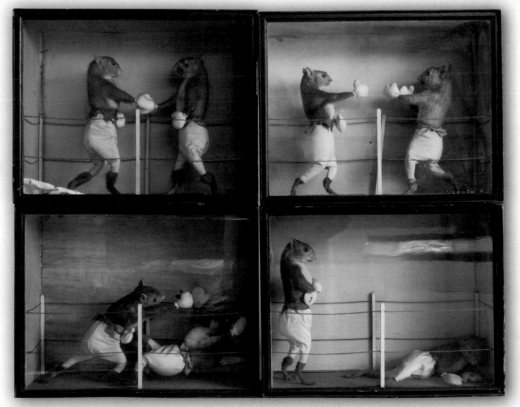

Four 19th century shadow boxes by William Hart & Sons of boxing squirrels, circa 1850s. This set was displayed at the Great Exhibition of the Works of Industry of all Nations in 1851. That the squirrels are wearing gloves gives a hint to their age; wearing gloves only became mandatory after 1867 when Queensbury rules came into force. These hung in the corporate dining hall at Goodyear Tires, the Akron, Ohio, tire maker, for many years. Each measures 14-3/4" x 19" x 7"; the set sold for 69,000.

Although Bill Crawley's collection includes strong examples from every genre of early American tools, you won't find it in a display case. His tools see action on a regular basis. Interestingly, his collection is influenced by an affinity for handles. Perhaps it's the curve of the wood. Maybe it's the wear patterns that are as unique as fingerprints. Or maybe it's because tools can be dated by the shape of the handle. He replaces badly damaged handles with hickory, dogwood, and mesquite wood, but does not touch historic tools that have value exceeding their use in the shop.

A WHOLE NEW PLANE

COLLECTING TOOLS

Bill Crawley lives a life as tough as his tools. As a young gunnery's mate for the U.S. Coast Guard, he didn't mind sticking lumps of C4 plastic explosives in his armpit to soften it for use during bitter New Jersey winters. As a director of psychiatric services, he didn't mind challenging an insensitive prescription or teaching nurses how to defend themselves from an attack. As a family member, he didn't mind spending days in the 100-plus-degree heat with his Uncle Burkhard, even though the old German gave him heatstroke three times. Uncle Burkhard introduced him to tools as a child growing up in Texas, but he also introduced him to the way of the craftsman.

"I like the old skills and a lot of these skills are being lost," he says. "Uncle Burkhard taught me there was a season for doing things. In the winter, you sharpen your tools by the fire. He also used to say: 'A pretty handle is pretty in the store, but you can't keep them in your hand.' "

Among the notable hand tools in Bill's collection include a Stanley Bailey Plane No. 4 with its original box; a 1940s-era Stanley Sweet Hart plane, retaining 80 percent of its original japanning, for which he paid just $7; and dozens of unusual tools that give a glimpse into how life once was. The

One of his favorite discoveries is this Stanley Bailey #4 plane, from circa 1910, retaining 95 percent of its original japanning. The value in its condition is about $30 to $50, but Bill likes it more for its ability to finish out hardwoods.

A small but useful collection of Stanley Bailey and Bed Rock hand planes are both on display as a collection and for convenience. Bill uses vintage tools in his projects in an effort to preserve vanishing woodworking techniques. The collection includes a Stanley Bed Rock #604 and a Stanley #4, with its original box.

collection holds a selection of Archimedes hand drills and a fantastic 1860s brass-plated hand drill brace made in Sheffield, England. He has an exceptionally interesting collection of adzes. The adze is one of humanity's earliest tools and was used for everything from scraping pelts to honing fighting weapons. Bill speaks fondly of his shipwright's adze or "American adze," his railroad adze, and his Connecticut hand adze, which was designed to hollow out canoes or burl bowls by hand. "Anything I can get for a decent price I buy," he says.

A collection of century-old broad axes hang in a group. According to expert (and Bill's favorite author) Eric Sloane, the axes were the most essential early American tool that turned round logs into square beams. "I have been after a goosewing for a while but haven't achieved it yet," Bill says.

Bill is the ideal collector. He enjoys the tools and understands that the most valuable ones are not the rusty farm tools still hanging in sheds and barns. It's the fancy, well-made tools that include quality materials that are the most valuable and profitable to collect, according to Clarence Blanchard,

president of Antique & Collectible Tools Inc., the corporation that owns the *Fine Tool Journal* and Brown Auction Services.

Blanchard holds a number of world records for selling the most valuable tools at auction, including the famed Sandusky Tool Co. 1876 Centennial center-wheel plow plane, which sold for $114,400.

Blanchard says there's not much required when caring for old tools. "Just keep them in a dry location," he says. "In the south with high humidity, rust can be a concern and a light coat of oil helps. In the southwest, dry air can be an issue with wood and so a coating of wax helps."

Bill keeps his non-historical tools in buckets in a safe dry space. He prefers working wood by hand, running it though his machines. He recently sanded a couple of boards of mesquite, which had been peppered with 22 bullets, into an attractive side table. When he's not making his own furniture, he's replacing the handles on vintage tools with various hardwoods ones.

"Mesquite is my absolute favorite wood to work with. It's considered a fruit wood and the wood is incredibly dense. The grain

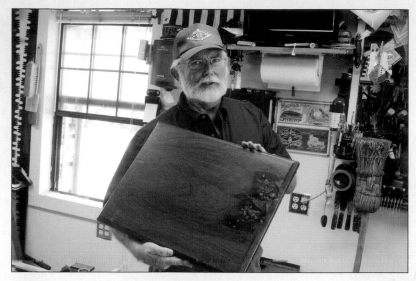

The top of a side table he's been working on is made of mesquite, but if you look close, you'll see it has a story to tell. The silver marks are .22 caliber bullets Bill discovered when cutting it down. "After I started cutting it in Zephyr, Texas, bored people showed up with lawn chairs to watch the job. It was a massive tree," he says. The rest of the tree is drying in a specially designed crib on his property, which is dotted with more than two dozen pecan trees.

This seldom seen adjustable plow plane dates to about 1890. Tool collectors go crazy for fancy examples of this tool. Top examples are inlaid with ivory or brass. Nice examples from the 1800s can be found for as little as $80 through dealers or on online auction sites.

is just beautiful. The tools I replace handles on are the tools that have no antique value," he says.

Remarkably, all of these tools are still in use. From the turn of the century saw vice to a pretty brass plumb bob, Bill turns to the dependable tools time and time again. They've even brought his family closer together. He and one of his daughters built a stunning cherry-topped dining table by working the wood together.

"She picked a Danish oil finish to bring out the curly grain," he says. "I'm really proud of that because her life is a part of that."

WHERE TO LEARN MORE

Mystery Tools: A blog devoted to odd or less obvious tools and how to ask for help identifying what you have; FarmCollector.com/blogs.

The books of Eric Sloane: From his home in New York, Sloane (Feb. 27 1905 – March 5, 1985) was a sign painter by trade who stoked his passion for history by researching tools and woodworking. His classics are fueled from a sense of American individualism and include *A Museum of Early American Tools*, a sketchbook, and *A Reverence for Wood*.

Antique Trader Tools Price Guide and ***Fine Tool Journal:*** Both are authored and edited by Clarence Blanchard, who also owns Brown Tool Auction. His tool guide is the finest identification book on the market and is available at krausebooks.com. *Fine Tool Journal* is a magazine for those who collect hand tools, use them, or just study their history. Blanchard is also just a really nice guy and I'm pretty sure his beard alone could take me in a fight.

Workshops store and display tools, but they also can be a trove of projects in various states of completion. Bill carved this bass and all it needs is a mesquite plaque and it's ready for the wall.

The father of Bill's uncle - a master carpenter - carved this broom from a solid branch of hickory. Strip by strip the wood was folded down, bunched up, and tied at the end to form a brush. The cord tying it together was made from the bark.

The inlaid side table and the Fox and Hounds game board was created by his Uncle Burkhard's father. Burkhard showed him how the right tools can help a man make a life for himself outdoors.

The most valuable knife in his collection was found in his grandfather's pocket when he died in the streets of Sulphur Springs, Texas. The Shapleigh Diamond Edge Knife has special meaning after Bill discovered two separate photos of his great-grandfather standing under a Diamond Edge advertising sign in the Hurdle & Garlock Hardware store he worked.

This group includes a hand brace (left) and a few Archimedes drills in the center, useful for drilling tiny holes. The bushing moves up and down, driving the bit at the end of the spiral screw shaft into the wood. Examples of the wooden block plane on the right may be found online for as much as $150 to as low as $5 at country auctions or flea markets.

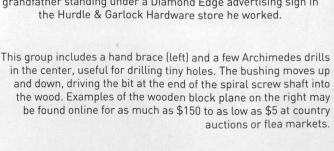

This Spiers, Ayr. infill plane is 8" l and sold at auction for $2,420.

$2,420

$9,900

This 18th century plane was made by Caesar Chelor, a freed slave living in Wrentham, Mass. It measures 4-1/4" w and has an ogee and round crown, an offset tote, flat chamfers and a round top wedge and iron. It sold at auction for $9,900.

This Lee's Stop Chamfer patent plane has a gothic arch type with arch design on both the nose plate and cap and an adjustable nose plate. It sold at auction for $9,350.

$9,350

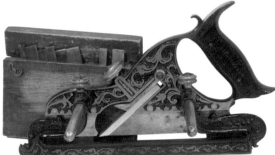

$11,000 A truly excellent Stanley No. 43 Hook miller's patent plane. This is the earliest type with the handle hook and the fence that has not been ground out for the filletster bed, as was done on the No. 41. The japanning is 95 percent complete and bright and the tool is accompanied by 10 cutters in the original box. The set sold for $11,000 at auction.

$114,400

Mantiques Fact: This is the most valuable mantique tool in the world. This Sandusky Tool Co. 1876 Centennial center-wheel plow plane sold for $114,400 at the 24th Brown Tool Auction.

$11,550

This great filletster plane was made by W. L. Epperson of Louisville, KY, in 1855. Epperson made planes before the Civil War and his planes are very rare. This is the only filletster known and it sold at auction for $11,550.

Charles Miller's 1872 patent was his first plow plane and his No. 50 was only offered for a couple of years prior to the Stanley 41. Retaining 90 percent of the original copper wash, the plane sold at auction for $9,350.

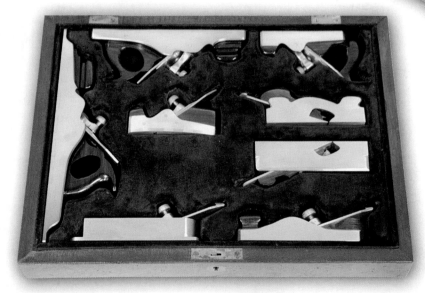

Excellent Stanley No. 1 Sweet Hart bench plane in the original box with two-sided The Genuine Stanley Bailey Plane store tag. It sold at auction for $3,190.

This set of eight planes was made by master craftsman Robert Baker in 1985 and runs the gamut from the rabbet to jointer. This is set No. 1 of 3 made for Ken Roberts. The other two sets are in England, one in a private collection and the other in a museum. It sold at auction for $25,300.

This Stanley No. 9 cabinetmaker's block plane, still in its original box and in simply awesome condition, sold for $3,520 at auction.

This Stanley No. 42 Miller's patent plane dates to late 1873. Retaining its original box, it sold at auction for $5,280.

This rare French coup Marc axe has a J. C. cutout head. It is 14" h, with a 12" edge, and sold at auction for $357.

This Lincoln axe was made by the Kretschmer-Treadway Co. and sold at auction for $220.

This decorated goosewing axe is considered to be in good condition. It sports a P. P. in a heart, a sunburst in a star, an arrow and the tail of the axe is cut into a nice decoration. It has a 7-1/2" head and a whopping 20" edge. It sold at auction for $412.

A vintage enamel sign for the Sirocco Tractors, surmounted with a thermometer and depicting a tractor and driver and inscribed "Warm Air Cab," is 12" square and can be found priced between $100-150.

This rare Stanley No. 70-1/2 slitting gauge sold at auction for $302.

R. Porter inclinometer has a walnut picture frame-like design that holds a pendulum needle that rotates a full 360 degrees. The etching shows two men laying up a brick wall with the aid of the Porter Plumb & Level Indicator. It sold at auction for $3,080.

A diminutive model of a workbench, John S. Powel, comes complete with tools and accessories bearing a brass plaque engraved "Miniatures of Merritt By J. S. Powel, Merritt Isl. Fl." It is 7" w and sold at auction for $200.

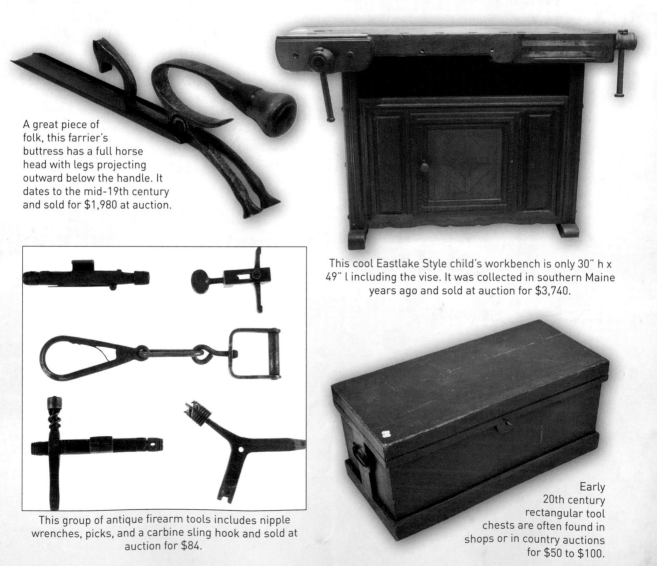

A great piece of folk, this farrier's buttress has a full horse head with legs projecting outward below the handle. It dates to the mid-19th century and sold for $1,980 at auction.

This cool Eastlake Style child's workbench is only 30" h x 49" l including the vise. It was collected in southern Maine years ago and sold at auction for $3,740.

This group of antique firearm tools includes nipple wrenches, picks, and a carbine sling hook and sold at auction for $84.

Early 20th century rectangular tool chests are often found in shops or in country auctions for $50 to $100.

A miniature walnut cased drafting set by William R. Robertson is 1-1/4" w and sold for an astounding $15,000 at auction.

This cool salesman's sample was designed to show dealers and farmers the benefits of owning a Frye's Steel Plow. No. 2. Salesman's samples are very collectible and this detailed example of a full-sized plow measures only 12" overall. It sold at auction for $2,420.

A great collector's piece, this Stanley Happy Carpenters 1939 window display shows each carpenter performing a different task and therefore using a different Stanley tool. This had never been set up until it was on display at the Stanley 150th Birthday Convention in Hartford in 1993. Includes the original display board from the convention. Board is signed by Charles and Walter Jacob, renowned collectors, Shirley Richard, Stanley/North family descendant, Stewart Gentsch, president and general manager for Stanley in 1993, John Walters, Stanley book author, and Clarence Blanchard, author, publisher, and auctioneer. It sold at auction for $2,130.

A small collection of vintage folding knives, some with ivory/bone handles, can be found for $20 to $40.

Colorful Stanley with Bench Plane and Curling Shaving lithograph by the N. Y. Metal Ceiling Co. It measures 9" x 18" and sold for $1,595 at auction.

GAMER CAVE
VINTAGE VIDEO GAMES

A s a new generation of computer programers, data specialists, and web developers begins to pay off their student loans, their attentions turn to collecting vintage technology. Surprisingly, this ranges from vintage console games and even computers. If this sounds too current to be called a mantique (or even vintage, for that matter), take a moment to think back to when you got your first console.

If you're a Gen X'er, then it was an Atari system. Founded in 1972, Atari remains the granddaddy of video game systems. Despite years of financial problems and a sea of much more successful competitors, Atari introduced the world to *Pong*, *Pac-Man*, and the Atari 2600 game system. The 2600 is hands down Atari's most successful endeavor as millions of families literally fought each other in department store aisles to own the console. The game introduced a number of pop culture tropes to American youth such as *Pole Position*, *Frogger*, and *Pitfall* and home versions of *Pac-Man* and even introducing Mario and Luigi, two characters who would go on to take center stage of the Nintendo console and solidify their presence in video game history as Mario Bros. Although millions were produced, the Atari 2600 is now a collectible and prime examples in the best condition often sell for more than $500.

The time line of collectible video games takes a noticeable dive in 1983, due to an oversaturation of really shitty games. Seriously, the quality of the games were so crummy that the influx of poorly designed characters

---

OPPOSITE PAGE: It may look like a coin-operated *Super Mario Bros.* arcade machine, but this cabinet actually holds hundreds of games. Tim installed a Nintendo Entertainment System equipped with a PowerPak NES Flash Cartridge capable of storing thousands of retro games, such as *Mike Tyson's Punch-Out!!*, the classic boxing sports game.

If gamer heaven has a basement, then this is it. The lifelong mantiques video game collection was assembled with standing arcade games and vintage consoles spanning 30 years. It can easily accommodate up to a dozen gamers and offers hundreds of games on discs, cartridges, or on an emulator.

and games shattered consumer confidence and sales plummeted. The collapse of the market saw revenues slaughtered from $3.2 billion in 1983, to around $100 million by 1985 (a drop of almost 97 percent), according to industry sources. The saving grace? The Nintendo Entertainment System home console. The system revitalized the market and consumer's imaginations. Vintage NES systems often trade at vintage video game shops for around $300, but like Atari, the true collector value isn't always found in the consoles.

Rare video game cartridges are where mantiques collectors are focusing their cash. That's how one collector, Tim, whose basement hoard is pictured here, got started. Like most collectors, he hung onto the games he played as a kid. He also took advantage of his dad's video rental business and kept all the obsolete Nintendo and Super Nintendo games from the shop. The other console games were mostly picked up through buying bundles on CraigsList, he says. "As for the arcade games, I found a collector around an hour away who restores and sells them for a decent price."

He rounded out his collection by crafting reproduction boxes for his vintage cartridges. "I spent a few hundred on plastic boxes and printing labels for the games I didn't have a box for. There are a few websites where people upload box scans.

TOP SOURCES FOR VINTAGE VIDEO GAMES AND MEMORABILIA

- CraigsList
- eBay
- Flea markets (get there early for the best prices)
- Yard and estate sales
- Fellow collectors: specifically the Killer List of Videogames, or KLOV for short, an online forum for sellers: forums. arcade-museum.com
- Consider attending a convention to play the latest games and find scarce cartridges or consoles: en.wikipedia.org/wiki/List_ of_gaming_conventions

A corner of the basement is reserved for retro games like Sega's multiplayer *Super OT*, *Mortal Kombat*, and *Defender*.

Tim has a 10-player set up so friends can play team-based games with one team of four to five players in the red room and another team in the arcade room.

The "red room" holds a set up of Xbox 360s and other retro consoles, as well as extra TVs for sports.

When I found that, I thought it would be a fun project to make boxes for everything." The memorabilia decorating the video cave comes from all over. "I found the Super Mario block at Toys "R" Us. The posters come from eBay, Valve Store, and some came with the games themselves," he says.

Tim's interest in arcade games is more recent. About 10 years ago, his interest turned to M.A.M.E., short for a Multiple Arcade Machine Emulator, an application that recreates the hardware of arcade game systems on modern PCs and other platforms. The software's only purpose is to preserve vintage games beyond the inherent obsolescence of their original operating systems and hardware.

"My brother bought the first one, a 4-player black generic looking cabinet which runs MAME. The MAME cabinet can literally run thousands of games," he says. "Even the Super Mario cabinet can run other games. I have eight arcades now and that is about the limit I want to have for the space."

It also happens to be his favorite item in the collection: an arcade version of the Midway Games classic, *Mortal Kombat*. "I did a lot of work on it, replacing the side art, replacing the monitor, and integrating the controls with an Xbox 360 so it can play the newest (*Mortal Kombat*) game."

For Tim, the arcade room isn't about quantity. It really isn't even about the quality of the games, either. It's all about friends.

"Lots of people have arcade games and some consoles but not usually something 10 people can play at the same time," Tim says. "It's pretty cool when someone mentions a game from their childhood and I have it and have the system hooked up to play it. One of my friends remembered some ridiculous thing in the instruction book for *Double Dragon 2*. I

The arcade room's gaming memorabilia includes a replica of the Master Chief's helmet and assorted figurines from the science fiction game *Halo*. *Halo* debuted in 2001 and the series has sold more than 50 million copies worldwide, for a total take surpassing $3.4 billion.

Rather than hold out for limited edition prints, Tim simply printed high-resolution images of his favorite characters on quality paper and slapped them with dollar store frames. Can you guess the game shown on the old school cathode ray tube television? If you guessed the *Super Mario Bros. 2*, you'd be wrong. It's Stage 3, "the waterfall stage," from Konami's 1987 classic video game *Contra*.

If Tim doesn't own the original box, he just makes a replica. Logos and decals are easy to find on gamer forum sites.

Sega's *Super GT* multiplayer arcade game was released in 1996.

had the game so it was fun to check out if his memories were what was really in the book and he was pretty spot on. I think it's awesome to relive memories like that with people. The main motivation for all the games and TVs is to make for a great party atmosphere and bring my friends together every once in a while."

$41,300

Bandai released *Stadium Events* in 1987. It was specifically made for the Family Fun Fitness mat – which spelled backwards means Epic Failure. No one bought the mat and that means *Stadium Events* is The Most Valuable Video Game IN THE WORLD. Nintendo thought it could turn the title around and it bought rights a year later. Part of the deal entailed pulling all remaining copies of *Stadium Events* from the shelves. That means that the only people who own this game are likely the people who bought it to play it, so when sealed copies come to market, collectors throw cash. How much? The last sealed copy of *Stadium Events* sold on eBay for $41,300 in 2010. Copies even appear online for as much as $75,000.

$1,556

Arcade video game *Ms. Pac-Man*, 1981, by Midway Mfg Co. This is a continuation of the *Pac-Man* line launched by Namco in Japan. This game offered better visuals and a new game board. Designed for two players, it sold for $1,556 at auction.

$30

This is Coleco's first video game console, circa 1976. It plays tennis, hockey, and handball and is a great piece of gaming history that sold for $30 at auction.

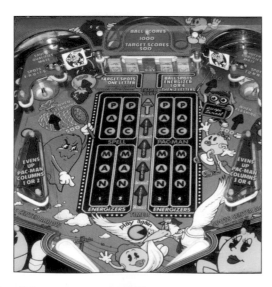

$1,213

There was no end to the *Pac-Man* family and this *Baby Pac-Man* arcade game from 1982 was made by the Bally Manufacturing Corporation, USA. It features an automatic electro-mechanical type, with two flippers, and represents at rare combination of mechanical games in a video game. It sold for $1,213 at auction.

Raise your hand if you had walkie-talkies as a kid. This electronic device was designed by Mego in 1977 to use with walkie-talkies and measures approximately 11-1/4" x 6" x 5-1/2 ". It sold for $60.

Tim created his own boxes for some of his vintage games, but you can find video game boxes at auction. This group includes empty Apple II computer video game boxes for *Aliens*, *The Black Cauldron*, *Leather Goddess of Phobos*, and ones not pictured: *Strategy Simulations*, *Wings of Fury*, *Lane Mastodon vs. The Blubbermen*, *Tass Times in Tonetown*, *Shanghai*, *The NeverEnding Story*, *Alf*, *The Chessmaster 2000*, *Space Quest*, *Captain Power*, *Super BoulderDash*. A fabric map with runes on it is also included. The set sold for $15 at auction.

Gaming conventions are great places to get used video games and other memorabilia. These games were for sale at a recent ScrewAttack convention in Dallas.

This poster was used in stores to promote the release of side scrolling video game, *The Empire Strikes Back*, released in 1982 for the Atari 2600 video game system. From the collection of the late John L. Williams, noted *Star Wars* collector, the poster, 24" x 36", sold for $478 at auction

"New video games" was the theme for this issue of *MAD*, and it seems Alfred E. Neuman has an anti-ballistic face! The background for this scene is an acrylic on illustration board planet-scape, while the "Space Invaders" were created using photostats pasted on an acetate overlay (included). The cover has an approximate image area of 16.5" x 22". From the *MAD Magazine* Archives, $299.

This would look awesome in a video game cave, despite the fact this original science fiction art by Jose Garcia-Lopez was done for an unidentified 1983 DC Comics project. The image area measures 12" x 15-1/2" and sold for just $57 at auction.

This is the original video game concept illustration art produced by Ivaylo Vakinov for the *Batman Returns* video game (Konami/DC, 1992). Released in conjunction with Tim Burton's second Batman feature, *Batman Returns*, this set of eight concept drawings measures 12-1/2" x 7-1/5" and sold for $155.

Resources

Auction Houses

AMERICANA

Hake's Americana & Collectibles
P.O. Box 12001
York, PA 17402
717-434-1600
hakes@hakes.com
hakes.com

Holabird.Kagin Americana
3555 Airway Dr. Suite #308
Reno, NV 89511
877-852-8822
info@holabirdamericana.com
holabirdamericana.com

Victorian Casino Antiques
4520 Arville St #1
Las Vegas, NV 89103
702-382-2466
info2008@vcaauction.com
vcaauction.com

Morphy Auctions
2000 N. Reading Rd.
Denver, PA 17517
717-335-3435
morphy@morphyauctions.com
morphyauctions.com

Rich Penn Auctions
P.O. Box 1355
Waterloo, IA 50704
319-291-6688
info@richpennauctions.com
richpennauctions.com

Showtime Auction Services
22619 Monterey Dr.
Woodhaven, MI. 48183
734-676-9703
mike@showtimeauctions.com
showtimeauctions.com

ART & DESIGN - ARTIFACTS & COLLECTIONS

Adam Partridge Auctioneers & Valuers
Withyfold Drive
Macclesfield
Cheshire SK10 2BD United Kingdom
+044 01625 431 788
auctions@adampartridge.co.uk
adampartridge.co.uk

Criterion Auctioneers
53-57 Essex Rd, London,
Greater London N1 2SF, United Kingdom
+44 20 7359 5707
wandsworth@criterionauctioneers.com
criterionauctioneers.com

DESA Unicums
ul. Downing 34/50
00.554 Warsaw POLAND
+48 22 584 95 25
biuro@desa.pl
desa.pl/en.html

Four Seasons Auction Gallery
4010 Nine McFarland Dr.
Alpharetta, GA 30004
770-781-2065
info@fsagallery.com
fsagallery.com

Hyde Park Country Auctions
323 Hibernia Road
Salt Point, NY 12578
845-266-4198
djnavarra@aol.com

Greater London Auctions
1200 Blalock Rd. Ste. #109
Houston, TX 77055
713-827-8886
greaterlondonauctions.com

Heritage Auctions
3500 Maple Ave.
Dallas, TX 75219.3941
877-437-4824
Bid@ha.com
ha.com

Jim Wroda Auction Service
5239 St. Rt. 49 South
Greenville Ohio 45331
937-548-7835
office@jimwrodaauction.com
jimwrodaauction.com

Leonard Auction House
1765 Cortland Ct., Ste. D
Addison, IL 60101
630-495-0229
info@leonardauction.com
leonardauction.com

Leslie Hindman Auctioneers
1338 West Lake St.
Chicago, IL 60607
312-280-1212
leslie@lesliehindman.com
lesliehindman.com

Mark Mattox Auctioneer & Real Estate Broker, Inc.
3740 Maysville Road
Carlisle KY 40311
859-289-5720
mattoxrealestate.com

Morton Auctioneers & Appraisers
4901 Richmond Ave.
Houston, Texas 77027
713-827-7835
larce@mortonhouston.com
mortonhouston.com

Nette Auctions
112 Beaver Brook Rd #7
Danbury, CT 06810
203-730-1404
netteauctions@comcast.net
netteauctions.com

Noel Barrett Vintage Toys Auctions
PO Box 300
Carversville, PA 18913
215-297-5109
toys@noelbarrett.com
noelbarrett.com

Premier Props
128 Sierra St.
El Segundo, CA 90245
310-322-7767
store@premiereprops.com
premiereprops.com

Saco River Auction
2 Main St.
Biddeford, ME 04005
207-602-1504
info@sacoriverauction.com
sacoriverauction.com

San Rafael Auction Gallery
634 5th Ave. San Rafael, CA 94901
415-457-4488
info@sanrafaelauction.com
sanrafaelauction.com

Specialists of the South
544 E. Sixth St., Panama City, FL 32401
850-785-2577
sospcfl.com

Treadway Toomey Galleries
2029 Madison Road
Cincinnati, Ohio 45208
513-321-6742
info@treadwaygallery.com
www.treadwaygallery.com

Wiederseim Associates, Inc.
1121 Yellow Springs Rd.
Chester Springs, PA 19425
610.827.1910
info@wiederseim.com
wiederseim.com

FIREARMS, ARMS, ARMOR & MILITARIA

Echoes of Glory International Military Auction House
1329 Harpers Road, #102
Virginia Beach, VA 23454
757-425-2827
info@classicfirearms
andechoesofglory.com

James D. Julia Auctioneers
203 Skowhegan Rd.
Fairfield, Maine 04937
207-453-7125
info@jamesdjulia.com
www.jamesdjulia.com

Rock Island Auction Co.
7819 42nd Street West
Rock Island, IL 61201
800-238-8022
info@rockislandauction.
com
rockislandauction.com

Hermann Historica
Linprunstr. 16
D.80335 München
+49 89 54726490
contact@hermann.
historica.com
www.hermann-historica.de

FISHING TACKLE

Lang's Auction, Inc.
663 Pleasant Valley Rd.
Waterville, NY 13480
315-841-4623
Sales@LangsAuction.com
www.langsauction.com

HAWAIIAN COLLECTIBLES

**100% Authentic
Aloha Shirts**
Vintage-Aloha-Shirt.com

**Surfing Heritage
Vintage Surf Auction**
110 Calle Iglesia
San Clemente, CA 92672
949-388-0313
Scott.Bass@
surfingheritage.org
thevintagesurfauction.com

MEN'S FASHION

**SC Baskin
Fifi's Finds**
etsy.com/shop/fifisfinds

Sewmanity
etsy.com/shop/Sewmanity

**Vu/Alyssa Duffy
aka The Vutique**
thevutique.com
thevutique.wordpress.com/
etsy.com/shop/TheVutique

PETROLIANA

Matthews Auction
19186 Nokomis Road
Nokomis, Il. 62075
877-968-8880
info@matthewsauctions.
com
matthewsauctions.com

ROCK 'N' ROLL MEMORABILIA

Backstage Auctions
448 West 19th St., Suite 163
Houston, TX 77008
713-862-1200
Access@backstageauctions.
com
backstageauctions.com

TECHNOLOGY

Auction Team Breker
Otto-Hahn-Str. 10
Koeln, 50997
Germany
+49 2236 38 43 40
Auction@Breker.com
breker.com

TOOLS

Brown Tool Auctions
27 Fickett Rd.
Pownal, ME 04069
207-688-4962
finetoolj.com

WINE & SPIRITS

Artcurial
7 rond.point des Champs.
Élysées F.75008
Paris France
+33 1 42 99 20 20
artcurial.com

Mantiques Businesses Near You

ARIZONA

Mancave Mantiques
7015 N. 58th Ave.
Glendale, AZ 85301
623-915-2283

CALIFORNIA

Mantiques Vintage Radios
11125 Woodside Ave.
Santee, CA 92071
888-716-1857

Mantiques
37390 Niles Blvd.
Fremont, CA 94536
510-585-3463
info@mantiques.info
Mantiques.info

San Pedro Mantiques
359 W. 7th St.
San Pedro, CA 90731
310-987-3697
sanpedroantiques@gmail.
com

COLORADO

Mantiques
221 W. Main St. #D
Florence, CO 81226
719-784-3131

MINNESOTA

Jim's "MAN"tiques
1113 Whitewater Ave.
Saint Charles, MN 55972
507-251-0050
or 507-272-2134
kidwell3@charter.net

NORTH CAROLINA

MANtiques
88 Marmalade Ln.
Cashiers, NC 28717
828-743-0004
352-467-2181

NEW HAMPSHIRE

MANTIQUERS
4 Union St.
Rochester NH 03867
mantiquers.com
porcelainneonsigns.com
webuystuffantiques@gmail.
com
603-948-1038
603-948-3456
604-969-1625

NEW YORK

Mantiques Modern
146 West 2nd St.
New York, NY 10011
212-206-1494
Info@mantiquesmodern.
com
mantiquesmodern.com
mantiquesmodern.tumblr.
com

OHIO

Mantiques
341 Rice St.
Elmore, OH 43416
419-205-8734
ernie@elmoreantiques.com
elmoremantiques.com

TEXAS

DFW M'Antiques
424 W. Davis
Dallas, TX 75208
214-941-4195
dfw_mantiques@att.net

Texas Coin and Mantiques
119 S. First St.
Lufkin, TX 75901
936-238-2793
texascoin.us

WASHINGTON

Mantiques Unlimited
5015 Auburn Way N
Auburn, WA 98002
253-335-1594
mantiquesunlimited@
gmail.com

WISCONSIN

Mantiques
111 W. Milwaukee St.
Janesville, WI 53548
608-563-5370
Mantiques111.com

**Double D Mantiques
and Collectibles**
11905 W. Dearbourn Ave.
Milwaukee, WI 53226
414-236-1255
*Get your mind out of the
gutter. It's run by two guys
named Dave.